What People Are

Conscious Women -

"*Conscious Women – Conscious Lives* is a handbook for any of us facing fear, loss and disease in our lives. These brave women have shared their stories in a way that gives the rest of us a roadmap to find our own sources of inner strength and guidance. During very frightening experiences and illness, it is hard to find comforting and healing strategies, and I recommend this book to help us effectively help ourselves and others."

~ **Marilyn Lake-Lee,** Designer

"The power to heal is within us and it starts with unconditional love. *Conscious Women – Conscious Lives* gets to the heart of healing and celebrates the joy of the pain and passion of living."

~ **Lorraine Seeley Buell,** Author of *SHIPMATES*

"A story can have a powerful influence on helping one find their path to success. *Conscious Women – Conscious Lives* is a collection of stories by women who have shared their journeys of healing some of life's greatest ills. These stories provide us with the hope and inspiration to persevere and triumph."

~ **Lisa Fraser,** Author *Parenting Letters*

"In my work as a body-centered psychotherapist, I've seen the value that writing can have to heal ourselves and another person. When we write about our life experiences and our triumph over pain and adversity, we demonstrate to others that we as human beings have incredible fortitude. That is the purpose of *Conscious Women – Conscious Lives.*"

~ **Patti Allen,** Body-centered psychotherapist

"In my work with past lives as a therapist, I have seen that when individuals remember their true nature as soul, they can surpass any hardship and overcome any trial. These stories make a major contribution to the work any healer does by proving that we survive beyond death and that we can survive spiritually even when everything else in our lives seemingly falls apart."

~ **Charles Richards, Ph.D.**, Author of *Karmic Relationships*

"Miracles can happen. *Conscious Women – Conscious Lives* reveals this through the revelations of women who have dared to share their journeys of healing some of life's greatest ills. My own life has been changed through both sharing my stories and reading about others journeys."

~ **Heidi Skari**, Author, *Red Willow's Quest*

Conscious Women –
Conscious Lives

Conscious Women –
Conscious Lives

Compiled

by

Darlene Montgomery

From the New Social Issues Series:
White Knight's Remarkable Women

White Knight Publications
Toronto, Canada

Published in 2004 by White Knight Publications,
a division of Bill Belfontaine Ltd.
Suite 103, One Benvenuto Place
Toronto Ontario Canada M4V 2L1
T. 416-925-6458 F, 416-925-4165
e-mail whitekn@istar.ca

Ordering information

CANADA
Hushion House Publishing Inc.
c/o Georgetown Terminal Warehouses
34 Armstrong Avenue,
Georgetown ON, L7G 4R9
T:1-866-485-5556 F:1-866-485-6665

UNITED STATES
Hushion House Publishing Inc.
c/o Stackpole Distribution
7253 Grayson Road
Harrisburg PA, 17111 USA
T:1-888-408-0301 F: 1-717-564-8307

National Library of Canada Cataloguing in Publication
        Conscious women – conscious lives / Darlene Montgomery, editor.
        ISBN 0-9734186-1-3
        1. Self-help techniques. 2. Women.
        I. Montgomery, Darlene, 1958-
        BF632.C65 2004   158.1   C2004-900381-X

Cover Art: "Summer Light" © 2003 Mary Carroll Moore
Cover and text design by Karen Petherick, Intuitive Design International Ltd.
Co-edited by Janet Matthews

Printed and Bound in Canada

Contents

Mothers and Daughters

Healing the Past

New Beginnings

Finding Courage

Dedication

This book is dedicated to my mother, Mary,
who inspired this book with her courage
in recovering from cancer,
to my daughter and friend Jessica,
and to all women on the healing journey.

Acknowledgements

I want to thank all of you who contributed to making this book possible by your willingness to share your intimate journeys through healing. It is because of your generosity of spirit, your creativity and courage, that this book has come to be.

Thanks to a my many good and true friends, Jane, Lily, Yolande, Janet, Thomas, Janine, Barbara Russo-Smith, Marlene, Barb Allport and Carol Lidstone who upheld the vision and provided both inner and outer support. I thank you with all my heart.

My deepest gratitude to Janet Matthews who helped open me to the world of stories. I want to thank my mother, Mary Montgomery, who has stood by me through thick and thin. You gave me true mothering and a home I needed throughout my life and for that I will be forever grateful.

There were many women who in their keen desire to be a part of this book were willing to extend themselves, emotionally, mentally and spiritually. A special thanks goes out to you for being so very helpful in maintaining the momentum of this book.

Thanks to each of you from my heart who gave their time to gestate your story and then invest your emotions, love and often tears to birth it through.

Thank you to each and every one who became a participant in creating this book.

A special thanks, to Sri Harold Klemp for both outer and inner support.

Introduction

Whoever survives a test, whatever it may be,
must tell the story. That is his duty.
– Elie Wiesel

Stories have and always will be medicine for the spirit. If so, this book offers a whole medicine cabinet of inspiration for women, from women.

What is the revelation the world is having over stories?

The relationship between humanity and story is as alive now as it has ever been. Through sharing our stories, we experience a continuity that reverberates throughout all ages of mankind and throughout all cultures. The profound affect of stories is that one's spirit can be immediately restored and healed and this is so with even the most embittered heart.

In compiling this book, I've learned that we are not separate from each other in spirit. We may live across the world from one another and still know each other's deepest thoughts and dreams. Through stories we recognize the commonality of our journeys, and that we are not alone but connected through the experiences we have. When we share our journey something happens; it is as if we must share our suffering, our trials, our wins and losses to complete the healing. We must give away something to realize the meaning of our struggles and victories.

As these women share their pain, fears, triumphs and realizations, it is my hope that you gain in strength and understanding so that you can take another step toward wholeness and move more fully toward your dreams.

My wish is that through reading, *Conscious Women – Conscious Lives*, you find encouragement, courage, hope, inspiration and a sense of connection to your own source of wisdom.

These stories are from all of us to all of you with love.

~ *Darlene Montgomery*

Healing Journeys

Healing may not be so much about getting better,

as about letting go of everything that isn't you –

all of the expectations, all of the beliefs –

and becoming who you are.

– Rachel Naomi Remen

Learning to Receive

When we see problems as opportunities for growth,
we tap a source of knowledge within ourselves
which carries us through.
— Marsha Sinetar

About a year before my diagnosis of breast cancer, I observed with amazing frequency the same first three letters on license plates while driving in traffic. The letters formed the word, ASK. When this continued to happen over and over again, I began to wonder, *What should I be asking for?*

There were many goals and dreams I still had for my life, so I had no problem thinking of requests. I'd always heard the expression, "Ask and you shall receive." But dealing with the experience of cancer was to bring out for me the deeper meaning of the word, ask, and teach me how to receive in ways I'd never imagined possible.

Prior to the first indications of cancer, I started having dreams of surgeries in heavenly-looking, inner world hospitals. Spiritual beings in white robes hovered over my body as it lay on the operating table. They seemed focused on my left breast. Then I'd be plunged into a murky darkness. I'd awaken from these dreams feeling sick and overwhelmed with sadness and fear. Something was coming. I just didn't know when, where, or how it would manifest physically. But I sensed that my dreams were preparing me for the worst.

In January 2002, I scheduled a routine mammogram around the time of my birthday. It revealed suspicious-looking calcified clusters in my left breast. A biopsy showed that these calcifications were formed around cancer cells. I immediately scheduled appointments with a surgeon and an oncologist. They told me that my cancer was the high-grade, aggressive type in the milk ducts of the breast. It could be removed through a lumpectomy, but the surgeon warned that this procedure isn't always successful, because the tumor was growing in the shape of tree branches, like moss through the milk ducts, and not a confined lump.

As it turned out, I wound up having a total of four surgeries in three months, culminating in a mastectomy. Each step along the way of this journey was fraught with difficult decisions and confusing and conflicting information. But in spite of all the surgeries (with a fifth one still necessary to finish the breast reconstruction), I was one of the fortunate ones. My cancer was the noninvasive type and did not require follow-up chemotherapy or radiation.

This whirlwind of life-changing and life-threatening experiences literally brought me to my knees. My husband, Allen, did everything humanly possible to help me. Although I'd had many friends in my life, now I needed more love and support than he could provide. Also, Allen's job required traveling, so I needed help with meals, the pets, getting to and from doctors' appointments, and caring for my wounds and myself.

Because I'm an inspirational book author, I've traveled all over the world and formed many friendships along the way. As I read through the literature I received from the breast cancer center, I came across an article that mentioned a woman who had formed what she called her Circle of Angels. These were friends and family members whom she could e-mail about her situation and who supported her in whatever ways she needed.

I've always been both a fairly private person and the one on the giving end. Rarely had I ever asked for help. As I looked over my original message about *asking*, I realized I felt unworthy. My needs and problems seemed so miniscule in comparison to others. How could I justify asking anyone to help me? I now realized that my lesson in having cancer was in learning to receive.

I flipped through my e-mail address book to find the names that lit up for me. I poured my heart out in a letter, telling family and friends about the cancer and my first scheduled lumpectomy.

The response was overwhelming. Letters and phone calls poured in from almost everyone with messages telling me how much I was appreciated and loved. I was deluged with cards, teddy bears, and other gifts that expressed their eagerness to support me through this ordeal. I had the unique sensation of knowing what it might be like to be there at my own eulogy.

Locally my Circle of Angels set up a schedule to cook and bring meals to our house. This would allow Allen to focus on taking care of me instead of having to cook and shop for food. Friends also set up times to stop by and check on me when my husband was gone, to take care of the pets, and to give me rides to medical appointments. Their care and assistance went on for the months of surgeries and recovery periods.

My Circle of Angels, as it turned out, extended into the invisible worlds as well. Before I was to have my third surgery in two months, I came down with the flu. I was very weak and was unsure about proceeding with the operation. I remembered the license plate message "Ask" and decided to ask God for a sign about whether to cancel the surgery or not.

The week before, our Saturday newspaper had carried an article titled, "Time halts in waiting room when loved one is in surgery." I had read this article and appreciated the reporters perspective. Now, my surgery was scheduled for Monday, and I was feeling extremely sick, wondering if I could recover enough to proceed. It was Saturday and my husband brought in the newspaper in its plastic wrapper. He handed it to me on the couch, where I rested, and I started looking through it. Then I noticed that the paper contained the exact same article about surgery as the week before. In fact, this brand new, freshly delivered newspaper was last week's edition! It seemed that an inner Circle of Angels had been at work to bring me the answer to the question I had asked. Yes, I was supposed to have this surgery as scheduled.

As it turned out, having the surgery was all in divine order. The surgery revealed that the tumor was larger than anyone had foreseen. And a fourth surgery had to be scheduled upon the heels of the third one. With the tumor as aggressive as it was and my husband's vacation days dwindling, time was of the essence.

All along, I had been writing e-mails to my Circle of Angels, taking them on my journey with me. Each letter brought back an outpouring of response with encouragement and information from others who had gone through similar experiences. One friend in California sent me a beautiful pin and earring set of a multihued butterfly. In the accompanying card she called me a Butterfly Warrior – one who had both strength and courage. Another friend in Iowa wrote about how I had received a Divine Kiss in the form of cancer as a catalyst for spiritual growth.

I made two requests to my Circle of Angels. First, I asked each to write or call to tell me what unfinished business I still had with them. I wanted lots of tethers to this physical world before I went into the surgeries so my subconscious mind wouldn't sabotage me into thinking I had no good reasons for returning. The answers I received were really wonderful. People reminded me of things I said I'd do for and with them. They reminded me of ideas for future projects I'd shared with them. They left no doubt that I had a multitude of reasons to keep living and serving life on this planet.

The second request I made was for each member of the Circle of Angels to share what his or her vision of me was. How did they see me in the future? Again, they came through with imagination and persistence. Their inner visions provided me with positive messages and hope for good things to come.

Through the Circle of Angels I formed true friendships with family members. Distance and lack of contact had caused us to grow apart. Cancer now reunited us. During the surgical procedures and their difficult aftermaths, my Circle of Angels held me in their hearts and prayers and sustained me.

I had to learn how to ask. I had to learn that asking means surrendering to what life brings and trusting that whatever comes your way is perfectly designed for you. I had to learn that I was worthy of receiving and that when others give, they grow and glow. I had to learn that on some spiritual level, I had even asked for cancer in my life, because this was how God would shower me with divine love and teach me to receive it.

I asked my Circle of Angels to think about who they would want to be in their own Circle of Angels. Then I encouraged them to tell those people right away how much they loved and appreciated them. Cancer had taught me that life is too short to wait to tell people that you love and need them. One of my last letters to my Circle of Angels included a poem that expressed some of the gifts that cancer brought to me. My sister-in-law copied the poem and gave it to her friends. One woman became so inspired by it that she named me as a cancer survivor she was running for in a charity event.

I share the poem now in hopes that my lessons and blessings will grace and illuminate the lives of others.

~ Linda C. Anderson

Holding Hands with Cancer

I have held hands
with cancer.
It has multiplied
like loaves and fishes
and fed many more people
than I could have
ever imagined.

I have held hands
with cancer.
It has touched my face
with its Divine Kiss
And drawn my attention
to the gifts that
illness has to offer.

I have held hands
with cancer.
And it has walked with me
over the bridge of despair.
It has released me –
a butterfly warrior –
Back into the golden sky.

~ *Linda C. Anderson,* 2002

My Favorite Year

*And so the mystery remains that we have sorrow
so we can understand joy; failure so we can
recognize success; pain, so we can relish pleasure.
Somehow, built into the mystery of this duality
in life is a blueprint for growth that has
the potential for shaping us.*
– Antoinette Bosco

Saturday, June 14th 2003 began unfolding for my little family like every other Saturday at our cottage just outside Toronto. It was early afternoon and I'd been chatting on the phone with my sister in B.C. As we visited, I stretched out on a swing and gazed at the gorgeous canal our cottage faces. Suddenly, Cindy's voice disappeared; we'd lost the cell signal. Pulling myself out of the swing, I went inside to where my husband Rob and our 12-year-old daughter Lauren were preparing lunch. When my phone rang again, expecting it to be Cindy I laughingly answered, "I guess we were cut off." But the voice on the other end was not Cindy – it was my new boss at the radio station where I had been co-host of a popular morning show for fourteen and half years.

In a voice shaking with nerves, she said, "Um, I'm just calling to tell you Erin, that you don't have to come home from the cottage tomorrow. We're going to let your partner do the show alone for a week, and then we're bringing in a new morning show." I was stunned as the meaning of her words slowly sunk in. My boss of one month was bringing in the team she had worked with at another radio station. Bob and I would no longer be needed for mornings. I had just been fired from the job I loved.

I told her we had to come back for Lauren's school on Monday anyway. And with that, my fourteen-and-a-half years with this station were over. With one phone call at the cottage on an otherwise lovely Saturday afternoon. When I hung up, the tears began pouring, and there was nothing I could do to stop them.

Over the next few weeks I cried a lot, overwhelmed by feelings of sadness, bitterness and anger, and a complete inability to understand this decision. We were a very successful morning team, and had enjoyed many years of tremendous listener support. As well, we were second overall in the competitive Toronto market. It simply made no sense.

During those first truly awful days, Rob and Lauren comforted me as best they could, but they too were fearful about our future. Would we have to move? Would we have to sell the cottage we had lovingly renovated? With one phone call our lives had been turned upside-down. As we drove back to Toronto the next day we discussed perhaps moving to B.C. where my parents and one of my three sisters live. Toronto and my career had been linked since the day I moved here twenty years earlier; I knew for sure I couldn't stay if I wasn't in radio.

As it turned out, I couldn't even stay another week. I was inundated with phone calls from television stations and newspaper reporters, well-meaning friends and associates wondering what the heck had happened. It was all simply too much. I had to get away, so by Tuesday I was on a plane to B.C. Nevertheless my firing was featured on the Monday evening television news. Then Tuesday morning at the airport, I was floored when I opened the newspaper and found my face, and my story. Not only had I lost my job, it was all so public, and terribly humiliating. The radio station was telling the media they felt they needed a "hipper" morning show. I guess I was the victim of a hip replacement!

My week in Kelowna with my parents was unbelievably painful – and I mean that literally. My body reacted to the situation by creating enormous pain in my neck, to the point where I could barely turn my head. An acupuncturist and chiropractor provided some relief, but what I really needed was relief from the stress and shock, something only time would provide. Mom and Dad did their best to console me with a combination of tenderness and stoic prairie wisdom. They reminded me I wasn't the first person to lose a job, and I wouldn't be the last. But it was hard for them to understand the enormity of my loss. I hadn't simply lost a job. I'd lost most of my friends – the "family" with whom I worked. I'd lost a position in the community I held very dear. I had been very publicly fired, and was now the subject of hundreds of e-mails and postings at the radio station's website. Listeners, as stunned as I was at the change, demanded to have me back. Some were now even offering up reasons for my firing, all of which were wildly untrue and often very hurtful. I blamed no one, but it was all just impossible to fathom. My self-esteem plummeted to an all time low.

Toughest of all, I'd lost my listeners – the people with whom I'd built a relationship for the past fourteen years. The people who had been there as I broadcast from home for three months after the birth of my baby. The people who had cheered me on as I raised money for charity by shaving my head at the Eaton Center. The people who wrote and called and shared their lives with me. I'd lost touch with them, and that was the hardest part of all.

But then something amazing happened. When I returned home and checked my e-mails, there were 1500 new messages waiting in my inbox! They had subject lines like, "What happened???" and "I can't believe you're gone". "How will I start my day now?" and "Hope you're well." As I began reading them, from one after the other I received an outpouring of support and kindness that overwhelmed me. Three months earlier, I had begun writing a daily journal at my own website, and now, by wonderful serendipity, it meant I could remain in touch with my audience on a daily basis, even though I wasn't on the airwaves. I was so touched at their response, and so very grateful.

June became July and still, Rob and I wondered what we were going to do. I was more fortunate than many people who are "downsized"; my contract had two years still to go, and I would continue to be paid for another year. But we had to look to the future. We had a realtor look at our cottage, and notified our agent in Toronto we might be selling our home. Crushed, and with a heavy heart, I began preparing to not only leave Toronto, but to end my career in broadcasting. I was doing my best to be positive and look ahead, but it was with great fear, worry and enormous sadness. And then the newspaper article broke that changed everything in one day.

The weekend after Canada Day, I received an e-mail from a writer at the *Toronto Star*. He was putting together a story about listeners' reaction to my firing, and wanted to interview me. Rob and I decided it was time to tell my story. Prior to this we'd been extremely cautious, lest we bite the hand that had promised to feed me for another year. Still careful, I answered his questions via cell phone as we drove to Ottawa for a weekend away. The Star's Ottawa photographer met us as we took a charter trip through the Rideau Canal, and photographed me sitting on the bow of the boat, smiling broadly. On July 9th the story broke on the front page of the Arts & Entertainment section. The headline read: *"Fans Comfort Jilted Davis"*, and the story and picture said it all. Public reaction to the station's decision had been loud and angry, while my response had been to find comfort with my family, to try and enjoy the gift of a summer off, and to look ahead to the future – possibly pursuing my aspirations to do television full-time. Between 1999 and 2001, I had hosted a TV show on a community station, and had always dreamed of doing it again.

Response to the article was swift and incredible. Overnight, my inbox swelled to 4000 waiting messages, as former listeners learned I had a website. I felt a sincere need to thank them for pouring out their hearts to me, for offering support, for needing to let me know how many years we'd spent mornings together, and what it had meant to them. It took until September, but after spending an average three hours a day on it, I finished answering every e-mail.

That article signaled the turning of the tide. The first amazing thing that happened was an e-mail entitled "Job Offer!" from Jeff, a talent agent, asking if I had an agent. I didn't. He'd just come out of a planning meeting with a manager at the W *Television Network*. They'd been discussing a new live phone-in talk show to air nationally in the fall. But who should host it? As they listed the attributes they wanted in a host, as Jeff tells it they both said "Erin Davis!"

The show's format was exactly what I'd envisioned doing. It would be live and spontaneous, with liberal doses of humor and heart. I was literally jumping up and down when I got off the phone with Jeff, having told him how perfectly I felt I would fit the show. I realized now I wasn't finished – I was only beginning!

A few days later I got another amazing e-mail, from *Ross Petty Productions*. Every December Ross mounts a large-scale broad musical comedy called a "pantomime" at the historic Elgin Theatre. Legendary for their silliness and great humor, they're good old family fun. His e-mail said, "We know you've done some singing - would you be interested in auditioning for the role of Fairy Godmother in this year's panto *Cinderella?*"

When I opened that message I doubled over, hooting with laughter. "Rob!" I called, "come here, you've gotta hear this!" Then we both laughed and hugged. What a perfect ending to a perfectly horrible chapter in our lives. Here were two amazing opportunities: the national television I had dreamed of doing – and this wonderful stage role, singing and

Conscious Women, Concious Lives

27

acting and having great fun. It would be eight shows a week in addition to my new TV job. I knew I needed to enjoy every moment left of my summer off, as my leisure time was going to quickly come to an end. And then we called both realtors – and said, "We're staying."

September 25th was a day filled with symmetry and magic. The *Globe & Mail*'s arts supplement announced that 'Erin Davis' would be playing the Fairy Godmother in the upcoming production of "*Cinderella*, the Sparkling Family Musical". That same evening, the W *Network* held its annual launch party to announce the fall lineup, and W *Live with Erin Davis* headlined the night. One more little note; September 25 was my last day before turning 41. I jokingly told my friends and family, "If life begins at 40, I'm just getting in under the wire!"

On October 27, the day of our first live national broadcast, I awoke at 5:00 am. It was early, but not nearly as bad as the 4:00 am alarms I endured for twenty years of morning radio! I can honestly say the first show was a true out-of-body experience for me. As I sat in the makeup chair being pampered and styled, I watched the clock, ("T-minus 90 minutes...I wonder if Mom and Dad are getting up to watch in B.C.") and tried hard to still the butterflies that seemed the size of dragons. The show – featuring songstress Sarah McLachlan – went off without a hitch.

Two weeks later rehearsals began for "Cinderella" – six days a week, eight hours a day. They accommodated my TV hours and I joined rehearsals by 1:00 pm, but it made for some very long days, with no days off from November 11th until Christmas week. I knew while I was spending my summer sleeping-in that one day I'd have to pay! Boy, was I right.

On opening night I was choked up with overwhelming emotions. After all this year had brought, I suddenly found myself on a huge Toronto stage, wearing a silver gown, waving a magic wand and singing a song called "Believe in Yourself". Originally from "The Wiz", it could have been written just for me. There were many moments as I sat in the quiet of my dressing room, I'd look in the mirror at this Fairy Godmother and say, "You did it. You really did it."

"*Cinderella*: The Sparkling Family Musical" was one of Ross Petty's biggest ticket sellers in years. The whole experience was capped off by a review in the *Globe & Mail* calling mine "the surprise performance of the evening". I never stopped being just a little surprised each night myself. Cinderella's dream came true, and so did mine.

My Favorite Year comes with a wonderful happy ending. My journal at www.erindavis.com continues to be visited by nearly a thousand people daily, and I still receive an average of 50 e-mails a day from it. And yes, I still answer them all. W *Live with Erin Davis* has just been renewed for another season on the W *Network*, and best of all, I've proven that just as so many of the letters that came my way this year said, "When God closes a door, He opens a window." Like most lessons, it wasn't an easy one to learn, but I am so grateful for having been given the lesson of a lifetime.

~ *Erin Davis*

Cleansing by Fire

God is burning out of you everything
which is unlike himself.
– Mother Teresa

At a conscious level, I couldn't explain why that Christmas of 1985 I wasn't in my usual anticipation to see my family. Normally I would have been dying to get there, but I was stalling, taking time wrapping presents, phoning friends, without my usual excitement to start the four-hour drive. It had been tradition for my mother each Christmas to bake a pastry shell filled with ricotta cheese and almonds.

When my mother passed away a few years earlier, I decided to continue her tradition, so the first morning after my arrival I began to heat the hot oil needed for the pastries. Naively, thinking I knew what I was doing (I had made these before) I retreated to the bedroom for a few minutes to change out of my nightgown while the oil heated. Those few minutes changed my life indelibly.

Fifteen years later while reading the newspaper at a gym I discovered a feature story about a burn survivor Sam, whose face had been horribly disfigured. The headline read, "A Man Burned Twice." It described his traumas: shopkeepers slamming doors in his face, security guards following him through malls, a post office clerk refusing to give him his package because he no longer looked like his photo identification, then the isolation, choosing just to be alone, because it was easier to retreat from an unsympathetic cruel world that didn't understand.

I read the article smugly at first. He had burns to 23% of his body, I had burns to over 40%, surely I was stronger. But, I finished the article knowing I was inextricably connected to this man. I retreated to the empty steam room like a wounded animal, lay down and sobbed, praying no one would come in. I cried for Sam, knowing exactly what he would endure. I cried knowing there was nothing I could do to take away his pain. But I also cried for myself; because painfully I realized there are wounds that take lifetimes to heal if we don't have the courage to meet them head on. I had healed somewhat on a conscious or mental level, but 15 years later I was beginning a deeper phase of healing that was equally as painful; emotional and spiritual healing, bringing deeper unconscious wounds to the surface.

That morning, returning to the kitchen, I realized I'd left the oil on high way too long – it had exploded into flames. I was stunned to hear the fire alarm wailing. I ran naked into the kitchen and saw flames flying from the pot. They had begun to melt the telephone right above the stove and the wall was blazing with fire. It was December 23rd. All I could think was, "I can't let my brother's place burn down two days before Christmas!"

Grabbing the flaming pot by the handle, I swung open the kitchen door. Before I could get out the door, a huge gust of wind blew the flames from the pot onto my entire body. I remember feeling excruciating pain for a second or two, then nothing. With my body blazing, I ran outside and rolled in the deep, fresh snow. I frantically started scooping up armfuls of snow and running into the kitchen to put out all the fire on the wall. It didn't take long because only a small section above the stove had been burning.

I don't remember feeling any pain, just shock and disbelief. Fires or burns had never been part of my experience. I'd never known anyone who had been burned. Just to be safe maybe I should go to the hospital, it was obviously nothing, and they would treat and release me in an hour or two. I didn't realize those flames had traveled past my nerve endings inflicting third degree burns.

It seemed unusual that I couldn't put on my clothes because they were sticking to my body. So I decided to throw on a nightgown, my winter coat and boots and begin walking to our nearest neighbor at a farm about half a mile away. I don't remember feeling any pain as I walked. It's amazing what a body in shock can accomplish. But, the pain kicked in the second I arrived. I knocked on the door and blurted out, "Please help me." I must have looked like something from a bad horror movie. My charred face was burned almost beyond recognition and much of my hair was gone. Mary Steeds, my neighbor was visibly shaken when I tried to explain what had happened. The pain was overwhelming and it felt as if I would collapse. Ironically, Mary was also cooking with hot oil. Minutes seemed like an eternity before she made sure her stove was safe so we could leave.

I was amazed when the emergency staff at the Smiths Falls hospital didn't make me fill out forms first or wait for hours. Reality began to set in when they immediately made plans to send me to Ottawa by ambulance. I was being given morphine injections every ten minutes. It wasn't enough. I remember begging to have them sooner and the sorrowful look in the nurse's eyes each time she apologized that only five or six minutes had passed.

I remember arriving in Ottawa, a young doctor looking very serious, stroking a pen up and down my arms, chest, legs, asking me if I could feel anything when he touched what used to be skin. I could see the pen but felt nothing. When he finished an older, fatherly doctor stood beside me. He looked at me with great concern and compassion and said, "Remember, through all of this that your attitude will be everything." His words injected a million dosages of morphine into me. Perhaps he knew that was all he needed to say. He just sat with me a few minutes then left.

My most painful memory was watching my father arrive in the emergency room a few hours later. From across the room I watched a nurse pointing to my stretcher. He looked at me, burst into tears, hid his face, turned away for a few minutes, composed himself, probably prayed, then came and stood beside me. My heart ached with joy just to see him, but it ached even more because I couldn't bear to see him cry. That hurt more than my burns. So I assured my father that everything would be okay.

That night I was taken to intensive care, hooked up to life support machines and left – perhaps to die. I though it was really strange that the nurses left me completely alone. I was still in shock and had absolutely no idea how bad this all was. No one could enter my room without completely gowning up in sterile hospital clothes and wearing a facemask. Since infection is the number one killer of burn patients, I was suspended in a germless environment for the first two weeks. I saw only eyes and what looked like flawless skin gazing down at me. Many burn patients slip in and out of consciousness if they survive the first two weeks. I was never unconscious.

Minutes after the nurses left me alone I began seeing beautiful white clouds softly swirling above the door in front of me. This all seemed very natural. It looked as if many faces were trying to form in the clouds, but they faded as quickly as they appeared. Then to my right, about three feet away, up above I clearly saw my mother's face. She was glowing, radiant, smiling, emitting waves of love like an energy beacon. I marveled at how beautiful and tranquil she was. While on earth her face had been a mask of pain and worry. She had suffered four years with cancer of the bowel and had many surgeries before she died. There are no words to describe what I experienced in those few minutes. There was an all-knowing peace on my mother's face. I heard no words but knew she was telling me, "Everything would be all right. Everything would be all right." As her image faded, I fell asleep.

A month later, a friend Linda, phoned to give me moral

support. "You're really lucky you made it," she said. "Made what?" I asked. Naively, I still had no idea I had been close to death. All I knew was that "attitude was everything" and "everything would be all right." It was years before I told a select few people about seeing my mother that night. I wanted no one to belittle or discredit an experience carved so deeply into my psyche. It had been my greatest source of strength.

Fifteen years later I stood riveted before the painting "*Concert of Angels*" part of a Toronto art exhibit "Angels of the Vatican." Although painted in 1672 by Giovanni Battista Gauli, those unmistakable swirling clouds with faces of angels was exactly what I had seen that night in intensive care. I wondered how many poets, writers and artists have witnessed this other realm and struggled to bring it back to the material world. But there it was, my vision, larger than life. I now understood exactly what transpired while I was straddling the spirit and material worlds. We're always given a final choice if we've written painful karmic events into our life script. This was not a healing as I had believed; it was my pullback from death. My spirit knew I had chosen this, but my body and mind were revolting in anguish and grief. They were literally saying, "What were you thinking when you agreed to being burned? Are you sure you want to go through with this?" Those angelic faces I saw in the clouds were souls that had gone before me, souls who had faced a similar life and death decision, souls that had chosen to live out their karmic agreement. My mother was also encouraging me to continue. She knew if I chose to die, inevitably I would have to come back and experience this agonizing pain all over again. It was far kinder to give me the strength to continue.

I was told I would be in the hospital for a year and would require several surgeries. I needed extensive skin grafting to my left leg, arm and chest. Since your body often rejects the grafts, they usually have to be repeated many times. The entire front of my body was burned, so layers of skin were removed for grafting off my back, from my waist to ankles. For months these areas hurt more than the burns themselves.

Miraculously, the skin grafts all took the first time. The skin which surgeons removed from my body for each anticipated rejection was never used. In two weeks I was walking on my own. I wandered into the physiotherapy gym and began using the equipment when no one was watching. My brother made a special grasp for me that helped me raise myself up in bed. Once I started walking I began my own rehab, visualizing a time I would jog again.

By the third week the nurses asked me if I would visit a young woman in the room next door. She saw me constantly passing her room and didn't believe I had been recently burned. Her pain was so severe she had been in bed for four months with burns on 17% of her body. We talked about her life; I didn't encourage her to start walking. The next day she walked for the first time. Then I was asked to visit a middle-aged man with severely burned legs who needed encouragement to walk again. He too had writhed in pain for months without leaving his bed. When you begin moving severely burned limbs, the pain is so intense your rational mind cries out, "No, no, are you crazy, stop, stop! Something that hurts this much can't possibly be good." Unfortunately, it is. We didn't need to talk long; I think he just needed to see another burn patient walking.

After one month I was proclaimed well enough to leave the hospital. (I later learned an acute shortage of hospital beds had a lot to do with this.) My skin was still raw, I couldn't put on clothing, and I was in unbelievable pain. The doctors said it would take five years before my skin was healed and all the pain gone. I didn't believe them. They told me I would be in the hospital for a year, and here I was getting out in a month. If they said the pain would last five years they had to be wrong – I would show them. However, they were right – the pain was unrelenting. For the next two years I wore a Jobst suit, a skin tight pressure garment covering my entire body from neck to toes, including gloves, because both hands were badly burned.

The Jobst suit assimilated your own skin which literally holds everything in your body together and creates a steady even pressure. This became my security blanket, which I wore twenty-four hours a day. Whenever I took the suit off to shower each morning the pain from my skin throbbing was unbearable. I never asked but I'm sure the name "Jobst" referred to the patience of Job one needed to get through these painful years.

At first I was in blissful denial buoyed up by love and support from family and friends. I had never felt so loved and appreciated. Friends flew in, took trains, and arranged carloads and vans to visit me. I was inundated with phone calls, flowers, gifts, plants and cards. I think something arrived in the mail for me every day for at least the first year. I had been teaching Grade one that year and it seemed the cards and presents from my school sprang from an endless well. Without all that support it would have been so easy to just give up. But, anger erupted when I realized the pain really would last five years. I was on morphine for the first five days, then Demerol for five days then nothing. I was told no other painkillers could be prescribed because over five years I would become an addict. All I knew was that I wanted the pain to stop, even for a blissful five minutes, so I was angry. Why did these doctors think they could play God? They couldn't possibly know how horrible the pain was, or else they would give me something. There was many different types of pain; throbbing, burning, aching, itching, tightness as your skin contracted, then shocks that literally jolted my whole body as nerve endings began to grow back.

On the surface I was the amazing burn patient that all the doctors raved about, but below the surface I was an unconscious torrent of anger, fury and frustration waiting to be released. I began pleading, bargaining with God. "Please God, if you take my scars away I will do anything. I will counsel burn victims for the rest of my life. Just look what I did for that woman with the burned arms in the hospital. Please heal me God, take away my pain and scars."

I'm sure God listened the way a wise parent listens to a child. I've since learned you just don't bargain with God. There are things our spirit has chosen to experience to pay back our debts. God knows and honors this. God is not a puppet master. Like Pinocchio, I had to grow up spiritually and understand I was more than just a puppet.

When God didn't take away my pain or my scars, depression set in. I wallowed in and out of this for years. On the surface it appeared as if I was completely together – a regular Martha Stewart. Since I couldn't go out in the sun for five years, I buried my emotions in academia, plowing through a master's degree in educational psychology and then a doctorate. I was still in denial about why the fire had happened – it was easier to do something productive that took my mind off the real issues. Years later a friend said what she remembered most about me during this time was that I was always laughing. All I remember is crying and feeling like I needed buckets around my neck to catch the tears.

In December, exactly ten years later, I had a vivid dream where I watched a man being burned alive in a white coffin. This took place in a church with all his friends and family watching. Although the man seemed to quietly submit to his fate I was furious. I yelled, screamed, ranted and raved at everyone in the church. "Are you lunatics? How can you do this to him? Do you have any idea how painful this is? I've been burned, you haven't. I know. You can never, never understand how horrible, how excruciating the pain is."

I must have yelled for thirty minutes in this dream, releasing a torrent of bottled up emotions. I realized I shared the same fate as the man in the coffin. That summer I had the courage to wear an actual bathing suit, shorts and a T-shirt for the first time. The sun and water felt glorious on my body. With the help of this dream I had taken a step forward in my healing.

There are times when I still look at my skin and can't believe it happened. There isn't a day that goes by when I don't wish I could just have normal skin. But, with each year the scars, shift, change, readjust. Remarkably, my skin and spirit are still healing.

At some point, I realized these scars had become part of me – permanent badges of courage I shared with all burn victims, our testament to the strength and durability of the human spirit. I was not convinced any more I desperately needed a miracle to take them away. It was the worst of times, my literal winter of despair. But it was also the best of times, my season of light. I was no longer a puppet, now I was a real girl.

~ *Marina Quattrocchia*

Finding My Own Medicine

For the truly faithful, no miracle is necessary,
For those who doubt, no miracle is sufficient.
– Nancy Gibbs

Those who analyze such things, say children who lack parental love don't thrive. It was true for me – I didn't thrive, I didn't want to thrive. Specifically, I lacked the will to live. So when in my early thirties, I discovered my life might be over within a year, I chose to abstain from treatment. Instead I embraced death.

I had no close friends and severed family ties long ago, so it was easy to slip away from my urban life. I had enough money on hand to last a year, six months more than I figured I needed. I chose for my retreat Quadra Island, just across an inlet from Campbell River in British Columbia. I found and rented a small cabin by the Pacific shore at Cape Mudge near an old Indian village. I settled in with booze, music, books and death on my mind.

Some days were good, some bad. I walked and contemplated, cried and laughed. I sometimes met people around the area, but if they got too curious, I lied. Whatever came to mind was the theme for the day.

Some days I was sick and frightened of what was coming but oddly most days were filled with an uncommon feeling of serenity, of being cared for and nurtured from an unseen source. Days were spent wandering the shore and tidal pools where I watched the water people. Higher up in the meadows I took on wings and flew with the sky people.

I first saw her in a high meadow – a native woman gathering plants. "Medicine," she told me. I watched her as she gathered leaves, flowers and dug roots – stooping low to bury tobacco offerings in the Mother Earth. Her connection with the plants made me conscious of the tall, graceful, shaggy-headed plants circling my cabin. My landlord had told me to get rid of them. They take over and are just "weeds," he said. I'd put it off, couldn't do it, they seemed to be there for me, guarding me, looking for me in some way. I realized then these were the standing people.

The next time I saw the woman she was digging the root of the very same plant. Surprised by the synchronicity, I asked her to tell me about them.

"You've found your medicine," she said. "This root is good for the blood, good for tumors, this is your medicine." She handed me a small shovel and we dug maybe twenty roots together. For every root she dropped tobacco in the hole making an offering of thanks to the plant. She gave me some so that I could do the same. I began to feel connected to life, part of something greater. I began to feel the power of medicine.

Words were seldom required between us, she knew all she needed to know about me. That day she invited me for tea at her summerhouse – a tent beside a creek at the edge of the tree line. The tent was large and airy and filled with earthy smells. It was furnished with a cot, table and chairs. As we sipped our tea she told me that she had known about me before we met and knew that she would be able to help me. She said, "The grandmothers had told me this." It was simply understood between us that I would stay with her and use the medicine to get well.

I learned her name was Standing Woman, she was Kwakiutl, and I stayed with her for three months. She took me with her to gather plants for my daily needs, telling me their story, and how to prepare them. Afterward we would make the medicine together. Some days I wasn't well enough to venture out, and on those days she sat with me and cared for my needs with more love and tenderness than I had ever known. As the days passed I became stronger and more confident that I had ever been. I was deeply connected to the earth, the same earth that I had wanted to leave just a short time before. One morning, I awoke and simply knew that my disease was gone. I also knew that my apprenticeship with nature had just begun.

Now, some twenty-five years later, I walk close to the earth, and like her, I listen to stories the plants have to tell. They teach me their medicine and I pass it on to those who want to learn. Before she died, Standing Woman asked me to carry on her work. I cannot replace her but I can walk with people to help them find the medicine they are seeking.

Some want to walk this way, and some do not. For those who do, I am here in the meadow.

~ *Kahlee Keane — Root Woman*

(This email was sent to the editor of Conscious *Women – Conscious Lives* by her dear friend, Arlene Forbes. Chosen to be printed as is, it is an example of the strength we derive from our circle of women friends on one's journey of healing.)

My Circle of Friends

All those crazy nights when I cried myself to sleep;
Now melodrama never makes me weep anymore,
'Cause I haven't got time for the pain, I haven't got room
for the pain, I haven't the need for the pain,
Not since I've known you.
– Carly Simon

Hi All:

Throughout this year I've connected with each of you via e-mail, by phone, or in person, and shared with you all a bit of my physical healing. The healing actually began two years ago. February of this year I had to receive a blood transfusion, two units of packed blood cells. The transfusion saved my life. I had gone in to see my GYN for my yearly exam. My lab report came back with a Hemoglobin of 4.5. Normal hgb is 12-13. Critical values indeed!

My doctor looked me straight in the eye and told me that it would be criminal to allow me to leave her office without treating the low hemoglobin. HGB is vital component in the blood. It carries oxygen to all the cells, muscles, tissues, and organs in the body. The heart pumps the blood via the arteries and veins. So you got to have blood in order for this process to take place. She told me that I could have had a heart attack due to the heart having to work so hard with so little blood volume. Ok, she had my attention now.

I was pretty much running on empty in the blood department. My periods were so heavy. Actually, I was hemorrhaging every month. The cause of the hemorrhaging – multiple fibroid tumors located inside the uterine wall. There was one tumor the size of a grapefruit. I did my research and tried several alternative therapies to shrink the fibroids. I am seeing Dr. Lu, acupuncturist, massage, nutritionist, chiropractor, and even a family therapist. And last but not least the loving guidance of spirit.

The tumors did shrink, but not to the point where the bleeding abated. Now I had to make some decisions here, and with not one more minute to waste. My doctor laid out all the options. Surgery at this point was not an option because my body wasn't strong enough to withstand it. I decided to undergo a series of six Lupron injections. One shot per month. DepoLupron is a hormone used to treat endometriosis, fibroid tumors, and prostate cancer.

In my case, the Lupron would be used to shrink the fibroids by decreasing my estrogen levels because I am so estrogen rich. The estrogen is what feeds the tumors and assists them in growing larger. As with many medications, there are the risks one takes with side effects. This drug did quite a number on my estrogen levels for sure. I experienced a rapid drop in estrogen, and I became very disoriented, moody, tearful; and had occasional lapses in memory. One day I was driving home in my neighborhood, and I forgot where my street was.

Fortunately, I had my license on me and a kind man escorted me to my home. This episode really freaked me out! But I realized I was shown the way home again. So it was a blessing.

The bleeding started again, so after some adjustments (mainly my attitude), and the right supplements, medications, and loving support from Aubrey and Linda, I started back on the shots. The side effects worked me for a while but not as intensely as before. I had great reminders and encouragement from Linda and Deb L. "This is only temporary, you can get through this."

I whined and cried for a while. Every muscle and bone in my body ached. The Lupron causes major bone loss as well. Bottom line – I got through it. My last shot was on September thirtieth. I saw my doctor on October twenty-ninth for follow-up. My hemoglobin was in the normal range 13.5! Did I mention the shots put me into an artificial menopause? I knew what was coming next. My doctor broke it down for me. I was now a prime surgical candidate. Lord, I didn't want to hear those words. How many times had surgery been recommended to me in the past two years?

"Is there something else I can try?" I asked.

The lupron shots were no longer an option due to increase in rapid bone loss, and six was the recommended number of shots in a one year period. Birth control pill\patch was another option. More hormones! More risks. Time to face the facts, girlfriend. I told her I'd contemplate on the surgery, discuss with Aubrey and get back to her. I totally believe that my doctor is a loving gift from God. She's been hanging in there with me every step of the way. I trust her. I realized it was all about me accepting the gifts given and accepting the challenge to heal. I am so grateful I did!

I met with my girlfriend Linda the next day in a coffee shop. We talked about my visit to the doctor. And the possibility of me electing to have the surgery. The tears started to come. I knew I needed to have the surgery. There was such a mixed bag of emotions – grief, relief, sadness, and even joy! SWEET SURRENDER.

As Linda and I sat there in the moment of surrender, we heard the song playing on the radio. Carly Simons' "Haven't got time for the pain." Many of you know the lyrics. I sat there singing those words. Linda joined in too as I got up from the table and pranced over to the condiment stand for napkins to blow my nose. I kept on singing along with the song and I noticed that the two ladies behind the counter were singing and dancing along too.

This was our song of Liberation. You could feel it in the air. Spirit is oh so economical. It became quite clear to me that I "haven't got time for the pain." I went home and told Aubrey I was ready to continue with my healing. We called my doctor and scheduled the surgery for December 5, 2002 at Fairview Southdale Hospital. The surgery will consist of a total abdominal hysterectomy, removal of my uterus and possibly a (B.A.S). bilateral salpingo oopherectomy. Translation – fallopian tubes and ovaries will get the boot as well.

With these terms, it sounds like we've got a lot going on down there huh? And we have. All I know now is these organs aren't serving me anymore, and I am ready to release them with all the love they served me with in the past 47 years. I gave birth to two beautiful daughters, Renita, twenty-nine, and Nicole twenty-four years of age. I am so honored these two souls agreed to come into this lifetime with me as their vessel to birth through.

I feel so vulnerable right now. I'm learning that vulnerability means strength, surrendering and trusting. These qualities are what it has taken for me to receive the gifts of God's love. I've been practicing nursing for over twenty years, and taking care of others with much love and gratitude to serve in this capacity. I've had to take a look at how I've been loving and serving myself as Soul. Balancing out the receiving has been the challenge for me. Well ladies. I am ready to receive. I am asking all of you wonderful women for your continued support through the next level of my healing journey.

Thanks to all of you for your recommendations for healing therapies, kind words, hugs, and most of all for the light and love you have brought into my life.

Love to you all,

~ Arlene Forbes

No Gift Too Small

I don't know what your destiny will be,
but I do know one thing: the only ones among
you who will be happy are those
who have sought and found how to serve.
– Albert Schweitzer

It was the beginning of a fall day. I'd directed a musical circle for children that morning at a school in North York, Ontario. On the way to the bus stop, I stopped to smell the roses at the corner of the street.

Noticing what I was doing, the lady of the house called out, "Would you like some?" Although the petals were beginning to fall off the flowers, I accepted. Their fragrance was absolutely wonderful and reminded me of my grandparents' farm where as a child I'd fallen in love with the same type of rose.

A few seconds later the woman appeared at the door with a pair of shears, walked over and handed them to me. After cutting a bunch, my bus arrived. In another act of kindness, the lady flagged him down. The driver stopped and waited as I returned the cutting shears and thanked the woman sincerely, from my heart. I hopped on the bus and immediately gave a rose to the bus driver who smiled in return. As I made my way to my seat, I offered a rose to a mother with her child, then gave one to another lady.

After arriving at the subway station, while waiting for my connection, I noticed a woman breathing laboriously. She held a little ventilator and put it to her mouth to assist her breathing. In a few moments the bus arrived and we got on. The lady with the ventilator sat on a seat in front of me. I took the last remaining rose out of the bag. All that was left of the beautiful flower was a little bud with three tiny petals surrounding it. Even now the smell was absolutely intoxicating. I really wanted to share it, but thought she would think I was ridiculous to offer her a broken half of a rose blossom?

I took a chance and tapped her on the shoulder. I said, "This may sound strange but I feel that I need to share this rose with you."

Taking the flower from my hand, she said, "It smells incredible!" She held it for a while, enjoying the scent, then turned around to hand it back to me. I really wanted to have it for myself but quickly offered it back to her. She said, "It means a lot to you."

I said, "I know it means a lot to you too." We went back and forth like that for a moment. "No, it's for you," and back and forth a few more times.

"You don't know how much this means to me. I've just come from the doctor's office and I got the news that I have terminal cancer," she told me.

"Oh wow, oh my!" I said, "Oh no!"

I was totally floored. The streams of tears came running down our faces together as we locked hearts and eyes together. We held each other's hands with this love and understanding we were sharing, in total awe of this very tiny broken bud that linked us at that moment. One stop later she got off of the bus, streams of tears still running down her face but a little smile at the corners of her mouth. I looked in the bag that had held those roses and found one tiny petal at the very bottom. I felt so grateful for the gift I'd received to be able to share with another soul at a crossroad in her life.

When I arrived home I put that one little rose petal in a beautiful bowl, floating on crystal clear water. I enjoyed the scent that still lingered and the memory of a moment of love shared with a stranger. The rose was just a reflection of God's love and that would be with me forever.

~ *Yolande Savoie*

Living Your Dreams

Obstacles cannot crush me,

every obstacle yields to stern resolve.

He who is fixed to a star does not change his mind.

– Leonardo da Vinci

The Man of My Dreams

I was at an all-time low point in my life. Recently separated from my second husband, I had moved across country to a new home in Upper State N.Y. I was in the process of changing jobs, and was raising my three-year-old daughter alone. On top of that I was renovating my new house. The pressure of all this change was extreme. Then, while attending a seminar in Minneapolis, a longed-for dream slowly began to come true for me.

The seminar was a regular yearly event for my religion, ECKANKAR, which amongst other things teaches the importance of observing our dreams. At that time, I was paying particular attention to my dreams to find help and guidance for my situation. While at the seminar I had purchased a small journal of stories by people who'd had profound experiences with their dreams. One night during the weekend of the seminar I awoke feeling ill, and decided to pass the time by reading this little book.

I opened it to read a story by a man who'd been detained at the Chicago airport by U.S. Immigration, enroute to this same annual ECKANKAR seminar the previous year. The Immigration official had wanted to arrest him because his name matched a known IRA Terrorist. To make matters worse, the officer mistook the personal dream journal he was carrying for some form of IRA code.

Throughout the course of the interrogation, the officer asked the author of the story all kinds of questions about his dream journal. He regarded the author suspiciously as he tried to explain the importance of dreams, and why he kept a dream journal. His ideas seemed a little far out for the stoic official, but as the author shared the understanding of life he'd gained through his dreams, the Immigration officer's demeanor began to soften. Now finished with his questions, the officer left momentarily. When he returned, he explained that a picture of the real terrorist had just arrived by fax, and because the author clearly bore him no resemblance, he was free to go.

When I got to the end of the story, a picture of the author stood next to his name. I was stunned to realize I recognized this man named Patrick; at least he looked very familiar. At the time I worked for a software company, and thought I must have met him through some business. But when I showed the picture to one of my friends, she pointed out that Patrick was from Ireland, and I had never been to the UK for business. It simply wasn't possible that I'd met Patrick through my company.

Over the next few weeks, I asked everyone I knew if they recognized the picture of Patrick, but no one did. Finally, one night as I looked over my own dream journal, I began to recall a man I'd met in my dreams over the last year or so. I especially remembered his eyes. A kind of shiver went up my spine as I realized it was Patrick. I was stunned as I realized I had met him in my dreams many times, but not ever here in the physical life. He'd been in my dreams when I'd been lost or frustrated, to help me with directions, and reassuring thoughts.

I realized I had to contact Patrick, even if he thought I was crazy. Through Eckankar, which had published the Journal of Stories, I was able to obtain a way to contact him. I decided the best way to introduce myself was by letter. It took a lot of thought to compose just the right words. Being a practical person, it was not really in my nature to tell someone I'd never met that I had seen him in a dream, but I knew without a doubt I must act on this strong feeling.

In the letter I told Patrick I hoped he wouldn't think I was crazy, but that I knew him from my dreams, and that my letter was a test to see if he knew me as well. I included a picture of myself with the letter, mailed it, and holding my breath, sat back and waited.

Six weeks later I received an e-mail from him saying that even though he'd never seen me, or dreamt of me, he thought I was a nice person and should not be embarrassed about my letter. I was disappointed because it had been so clear to me I knew him. I decided not to give up, and carried on a very casual correspondence with him. During that time, I was in a lot of turmoil as the change in my life continued.

After corresponding for six months, Patrick invited me to Ireland for a visit. I decided to take a risk and go, after all, how many times would I have an opportunity like this?

After a long flight on the red-eye, I arrived in Dublin Airport at seven a.m. on a Sunday morning in May 1999. I was tired, and wondered what the heck I was doing crossing the ocean to meet a man I'd only ever seen in my dreams! As I sat reading a magazine and waiting for Patrick, I looked up to see a man with a beer belly approaching. "If that's him," I thought in a panic, "I'll just leave now by the back door!" Fortunately it wasn't!

A few moments later, a tall rather gaunt looking man approached with huge piercing green eyes. As I stood up and looked into his eyes, I felt that I was meeting a loved one I'd been apart from for a very long time. My heart opened immediately and I knew this man had walked right out of my dreams. Later I learned Patrick had recently suffered a gallbladder attack and had spent the last three weeks in hospital on intravenous. Over that time he'd lost thirty pounds, which explained the disparity between the picture I'd seen in the book, and his appearance now.

We decided to leave Dublin and do a little traveling in the country, where we visited some beautiful places. As we got to know each other, we naturally got closer and closer. It was while standing overlooking Killarney Bay that I realized I was going to marry this man.

On the third day, we went to visit some old friends of mine who'd moved to Ireland from the U.S. All the while, Patrick kept asking me questions about my hometown. He asked specific questions about my house and my yard, and they were so specific, I could not imagine where he was going with it all.

Then I learned that although Patrick is a very practical and pragmatic man, for some reason he'd packed his own dream journals to bring along on our little trip. He told me he'd reviewed his journals and had found dreams he now realized were about me. There was one where he'd walked into a shopping mall with the woman he used to live with in Ireland, and then walked out the front door with another woman with auburn hair, and a little girl with long blond hair. I have auburn hair, and he now realized the dream was of my daughter and me, and had foretold the future when he and I would find each other after many lifetimes apart.

My face hadn't been in any of these dreams, and that's why he hadn't recognized my picture when I first sent it. Patrick was now able to put a face to the woman in the dreams, and he knew it was me. He then told me the morning we'd met at the airport he had instantly realized he had been with me in his dreams.

We were amazed at how specific some of his dreams were. Although he had recorded them a few years before my house was renovated, Patrick related in detail the color of my couch in the family room, and specific details of the house and back yard. These were things he simply couldn't have known. In one dream, a guide had led him through my town in Skaneatles, N.Y. showing Patrick details of the town including a long pier that stretched out on the lake in front of my home. It was clear we'd both been prepared far in advance of our meeting. It was all written down – a soul contract we'd made with each other long ago.

Once I returned home our relationship continued to deepen. I flew back to Ireland twice more, and then Patrick flew to America to visit and meet my daughter Paige in person. The immediate bond they shared was startling, and deep. As a matter of fact Paige hardly ever wanted to be out of Patrick's presence. It was clear we'd all been together before. After he returned to Ireland, we spoke on the phone every day, and Patrick sent me some wonderful poems and cards. In October 1999, a year from when I'd first seen his picture in the little journal of stories, we announced our engagement.

I began work to get the Visa paperwork for a Fiancée sponsorship. Patrick came over to Skaneatles to stay a few months prior to our wedding, which was to take place in February 1999. Six weeks before our wedding, he flew back to Ireland to obtain his final Visa.

To our shock and horror, when he arrived at the American Embassy in Dublin, his passport was confiscated. He was told there was a multi-national criminal investigation underway regarding the same IRA terrorist from his previous experience in Chicago. The CIA, DIA, NSA, Interpol, and other agencies were all involved. We were terrified he might be detained indefinitely, and that our plans and dreams were all about to fall apart.

In desperation we began making calls to every politician we knew who might be able to help. I called some lawyers I knew in Washington DC who'd worked with Immigration, and asked if they could help. My friends and family advised me to hold off on sending out the wedding invitations, for fear this situation might be true! "After all," they warned, "do you really know him?" It was a real test for us.

Our beliefs included reincarnation, and based on our dream experiences and other confirmations, we knew beyond a doubt that our upcoming marriage was meant to be. This was just another test. I knew this man and I were supposed to be together, and so did he. Disregarding the skeptics, I held true to our vision, and sent the invitations out.

After two and a half very long weeks, Patrick was cleared. The American Embassy returned his passport and granted the Visa, and Patrick returned to me. On February 19, 2000, we were married in a fantastic Celtic ceremony. On that day, Patrick and I declared our love for each other before our families and friends. As I looked into his deep green eyes, the very eyes I'd seen in my dreams for so long, we exchanged our vows. I can truly say that dreams do come true.

Since then, we've adopted a little boy and are now raising our two children together. We both continue to keep dream journals, and continue to believe in the power of our dreams.

~ *Barbara O'Connell*

The Making of a Miracle

The more you praise and celebrate your life,
the more there is in life to celebrate.
– Oprah Winfrey

When I was teaching high school in Cincinnati, I ran a very special program in one of the most affluent schools in the state of Ohio. My program, called NOVA, was for disaffected students. This meant that these students were turned off by the public school curriculum for whatever reason and were achieving way below their potential. Some of them were gifted and talented, some were not. This population of students had been identified and grouped together.

The school hired me to create a curriculum for this diverse group that would cover various subjects including English, philosophy, literature and history, composition, and several of the fine arts. The students would attend specific other classes outside my program for science and math and a few other select courses. I was to run the program and monitor these students and their progress.

The goal for the NOVA program was to help move these students to a new level of success – both academic and social. Many skipped school a great deal of the time and disliked it immensely. A big challenge for me was to get them excited enough about the program that they would come to school every day and participate.

We had a beautiful part of the school all to ourselves in a

large circular classroom area in the center of the school. My students were a varied group, in age and potential, but the setting allowed for a lot of individual instruction and things got off to a great start.

To get the students excited about coming to class, I met with them one-on-one making big promises to them about what they would learn and how it would serve them in life. I felt certain that I could deliver my end of the deal if they would just come to class. If I heard through the grapevine that a student intended to skip school, I would often go by their home in the morning and knock on the front door or even their bedroom window. I greeted them with a big smile and made more promises of what their day would offer if they would just show up. Usually this was all that was needed. They would come to class to avoid having me come banging on the door at the crack of dawn.

When I got them in the classroom, what I delivered, along with the regular courses of study, was the highest measure of truth that I could possibly present. This stimulated and intrigued my students and caused a deeper, inquisitive side of them to awaken. I believe that one of the things that we can do to make our lives better is to practice the application of spiritual principles to help us keep achieving our dreams and that in this way we will someday fulfill our greatest destiny in this lifetime. I wanted to stimulate the students to do their best so I put very uplifting quotes on the walls that contained spiritual principles to live by – some of the quotes were from Emerson, Thoreau and other writers and philosophers. One of the student's favorites was Paul Twitchell, a writer who inspired me with his esoteric books. In a book called the *Flute of God*, I found these words that remained on my chalk board all year:

> *"We must know that the gift is made even before we see it. Consciousness must receive the gift before it comes into manifestation on this physical plane."*

On my wall I also put a couple of lines that have been very loosely attributed to Paul Twitchell, thinking that the students would find them outrageous, but intriguing.

"Miracles I can do in a minute. The impossible takes about three days."

I wanted my students to have a greater sense of hope about their lives and their own power to achieve great things. At their young ages, they had either already given up any sense of personal power or had never developed it. Life seemed pointless for many of them. We had many stimulating discussions in my class to help dispel this negative attitude of having no control over one's own life. We were discussing the fact that we may indeed have far more control over our own lives than most people think and that when we learn to harness our inner resources we can become both more responsible and more capable. The quote about miracles and doing the impossible in three days, pushed my students right to the limit.

"We can't do miracles and no one can do the impossible," they insisted. This, of course, was just the sort of debate I had hoped to stimulate. But on a Friday afternoon they were demanding and belligerent. They finally asked me to give then an example from my own life. I gave them examples from my past but they wanted to pose an experiment. They challenged me to do "the impossible" in three days or less!

I explained that when we ask for what we want and put it confidently out in the universe, amazing things can happen. There are some conditions, however. Our hearts have to be open to receive, we have to be willing to imagine it as if it already existed, and we have to be willing to do our part. I explained that we also have to be careful to be open and not trying to dictate the details. I always ask for what I want and add, "If not this, then something greater." I surrender the outcome with these words, so that whatever I receive is best for the good of the whole. Otherwise what we ask for might not be for our good, and we might be unaware. And if we use this technique of surrendering to "this or something greater," it leaves the door open for an even bigger blessing to arrive.

My students really wanted to make a contest out of this idea. They wanted me to think about something I wanted to manifest in my life, but could not or had not up to this point. I thought about it for a moment and then I remembered something I had been really wanting recently. I love new adventures and I had previously been skydiving, scuba diving and rock climbing. I wanted a new adventure, but it was one that I did not have the money to engage in at the moment. I had been dreaming about this new adventure for a while and I really wanted to get the chance to try it sometime in the very near future. But I had checked the prices and it was a lot more expensive than I had the finances for at the moment.

I told them that for me right now, it would be at least a *small* miracle if I could find a way to go on a hot air balloon ride. I really wanted this small adventure in my life. I had seen what it would be like in a film recently and I longed to be flying over the terrain in a brightly colored balloon. I could feel myself sailing over the rooftops and wanted to experience that grand sense of freedom and joy. I wanted to fly over the rivers and streams and see the treetops with full autumn colors painting the landscape. I described all this to my students and I said that maybe I would get an unexpected bonus in the near future and I would use it for my hot air balloon ride. They did not like this at all. Ah, I must already be *expecting* a bonus and then I would just say that it was unexpected when it arrived. They wanted a bigger miracle than a hot air balloon ride but it was the end of class so I could easily get off the hook for now.

"Never mind," I told the class. "We are dealing with miracles and the impossible here so we will all just have to wait to see what happens! I'll know it's a miracle if I get a hot air balloon ride, and you'll all still be stuck on the ground."

They laughed and that was the end of our time together on Friday.

That night I went to the coin-operated laundry in the area where I lived and while I was doing my laundry for the week, a young man approached me. He was selling raffle tickets for a charity called "The Neediest Children of All," and when he said the name of the charity it brought tears to my eyes. He showed me the literature and told me a bit about the charity. He had only one ticket left to sell.

I felt so blessed in my life. I loved my career; I had a beautiful baby girl; and life was sweet – even if rather tight on the finances. I had just moved and the expenses used up all my extra money. My bank accounts were down to nothing until my next payday. I had a little cash in my pocket but not much. Now this man was asking for part of my meager funds for a cause that I knew little about, but that had clearly touched my heart. I listened as he explained how this charity helped children. My own life felt so blessed that I wanted to help. I did not ask what the raffle prize might be since that was clearly not my motivation. I shook my head as I gave him my last five dollars until payday on Monday. I wrote my name and phone number on the raffle ticket and kept the stub. As he left I said, "How will I know if I've won?"

"Someone will call you," he promised as he waved a big goodbye.

The very next morning my phone rang. I had won the raffle. The prize? A sunset, hot air balloon ride over the Cincinnati river and city view! It would be the very next day – Sunday afternoon! I was truly excited about getting my little adventure, but was even more thrilled about the prospect of telling my students! They might never believe that it was not planned all along, but I would know!

That Sunday afternoon brought beautiful weather with it. It was warm, the sky was beautiful and the fall leaves were at their best. When I arrived at the appointed time and place, there was a big crowd. I managed to make my way through the people milling all around and went toward the brightly colored balloon already filled with hot air and tethered in place, peacefully waiting its passengers.

I approached one of the people standing near the basket of the balloon and told them who I was. To my surprise, I discovered that they were all waiting for me. There were interviews scheduled and a big send-off event was planned. I was immediately introduced to the media. This was a significant fund-raising drive and many charities had participated. The television stations all had reporters there and they wanted before-and-after interviews with me. They asked all about when I bought my ticket and why I had participated. I made it very clear that I had been hoping and dreaming for a hot air balloon ride, but I had not even known the potential prize when I bought my ticket. There were politicians, celebrities and me! I was showered with attention, treated like a superstar and given a very special hot air balloon ride – all for the price of my last five dollars!

That night, I saw myself on the ten o'clock news. I later found out I was on every station in the area. I was pretty sure my high school students would have heard about it too. And the next morning I was really certain the word would spread, as there was a small story and picture in the morning paper as well.

When I went to school on Monday morning, I told my students, "You have to admit, this is my dream and desire manifested in a way none of us would have expected." They could not accuse me of rigging the contest and by now they were quite intrigued by how this had all happened. They were ready to learn and to listen.

What I marveled at was not just that my dream came true, but that I received the "something better" as well. I surrendered the entire thing to Divine Spirit – and I had received an amazing hot air balloon ride, with superstar status, at a rock-bottom price. And it had all happened within the three-day limit, with perfect weather, full autumn leaves, and with a bonus of complete news coverage so that it served as a great illustration for my students of spiritual principles in action – all wrapped up in one beautiful package.

These principles work for each of us in the same way. They are universal spiritual principles. It is definitely best to apply spiritual principles in the spirit of love and detachment. Then add a dash of trust, complete surrender, and a belief that our greatest good is being taken care of at all times. To that, we simply move forward with a willingness to do our part, and we have a perfect formula for success.

~ *Anne Archer Butcher*

Finding My Wings

How do the geese know when to fly to the sun?
Who tells them the seasons?
How do we, humans, know when it is time to move on?
As with the migrant birds, so surely with us,
there is a voice within,
if only we would listen to it,
that tells us so certainly when to go forth
into the unknown.
– Elizabeth Kubler-Ross

Like so many other girls, my self-confidence growing up was almost nonexistent. I doubted my abilities, had little faith in my potential and questioned my personal worth. If I achieved good grades, I believed that I was just lucky. Although I made friends easily, I worried that once they got to know me, the friendship wouldn't last. And when things went well, I thought I was just in the right place at the right time. I even rejected praise and compliments.

The choices I made reflected my self-image. While in my teens, I attracted a man with the same low self-esteem. In spite of his violent temper and an extremely rocky dating relationship, I decided to marry him. I still remember my dad whispering to me before walking me down the aisle, "It's not too late Sue. You can change your mind." My family knew what a terrible mistake I was making. Within weeks, I knew it too.

The physical abuse lasted for several years. I survived serious injuries, was covered with bruises much of the time and had to be hospitalized on numerous occasions. Life became a blur of police sirens, doctors' reports and family court appearances. Yet I continued to go back to the relationship, hoping that things would somehow improve.

After we had our two little girls, there were times when all that got me through the night was having those chubby little arms wrapped around my neck, pudgy cheeks pressed up against mine and precious toddler voices saying, "It's all right, Mommy. Everything will be okay." But I knew that it wasn't going to be okay. I had to make changes – if not for myself, then to protect my little girls.

Then something gave me the courage to change. Through work, I was able to attend a series of professional development seminars. In one, a presenter talked about turning dreams into realities. That was hard for me – even to dream about a better future. But something in the message made me listen.

She asked us to consider two powerful questions: "If you could be, do, or have anything in the world, and you knew it would be impossible to fail, what would you choose? And if you could create your ideal life, what would you dare to dream?" In that moment, my life began to change. I began to dream.

I imagined having the courage to move the children into an apartment of our own and start over. I pictured a better life for the girls and me. I dreamed about being an international motivational speaker so that I could inspire people the way the seminar leader had inspired me. I saw myself writing my story to encourage others.

So I went on to create a visual picture of my new success. I envisioned myself wearing a red business suit, carrying a leather briefcase and getting on an airplane. This was quite a stretch for me, since at the time I couldn't afford a suit.

Yet I knew that if I was going to dream, it was important to fill in the details for my five senses. So I went to the leather store and modeled a briefcase if front of the mirror. How would it look and feel? What does leather smell like? I tried on some red suits and even found a picture of a woman in a red suit, carrying a briefcase and getting on a plane. I hung the picture up where I could see it every day. It helped to keep the dream alive.

And soon the changes began. I moved with the children to a small apartment. On only $98 a week, we ate a lot of peanut butter and drove an old jalopy. But for the first time, we felt free and safe. I worked hard at my sales career, all the time focusing on my "impossible dream."

Then one day I answered the phone, and the voice on the other end asked me to speak at the company's upcoming annual conference. I accepted, and my speech was a success. This led to a series of promotions, eventually to national sales trainer. I went on to develop my own speaking company and have traveled to many countries around the world. My "impossible dream" has become a reality.

I believe that all success begins with spreading your W. I. N. G. S.– believing in your worth, trusting in your insight, nurturing yourself, having a goal and devising a personal strategy. And then, even impossible dreams become real.

~ *Sue Augustine*

One Small Voice

You are not here merely to make a living.
You are here in order to enable the world to live more
amply, with greater vision, with a finer spirit of hope and
achievement. You are here to enrich the world, and you
impoverish yourself if you forget the errand.
—Woodrow Wilson, 28th President of the United States

I laid my pages in front of me and gripped the sides of the podium. 'Remember to make eye contact with your audience,' Mrs. Hollingsworth had warned us. When I looked out at the sea of faces below me, my tongue stuck to the roof of my mouth. Then I heard an unfamiliar voice recite the title of my speech. I let it speak for me, and the voice began to rise and fall with passion and the words I had written.

As far back as Grade 1, at least three times a week after school, after all my friends were at home changing into play clothes, I'd stand alone on my tiptoes at the front of the class printing on the blackboard. 'I must read aloud from *Dick and Jane* when Mother St. Zita calls on me.' That was the penance I wrote one hundred times for refusing to read in front of my classmates.

To my teachers, I was a pigtailed, hard-headed chatterbox who refused to comply with their demands. They didn't know that I stuttered when I read to an audience – any audience. During reading class, I sat envying Carol Brent who read *Dick and Jane* flawlessly. In bed, I prayed to the Little Flower to make me read like Sandra Lefebvre who was brave enough to take deep breaths after periods.

Once, in Grade 1, before I realized the proportion of my stuttering, I tried to read aloud for Mother St. Zita. My heart jumped so violently against my chest that I could manage only shallow breaths. They bumped into my words, with the result that what tumbled out of my mouth was one long, ugly blob of sound. 'Dick' and 'Spot' stayed lodged in my throat and never came out at all. All the first-graders laughed and clapped their hands in glee. Mother St. Zita yanked off her glasses and wailed, "Oh Mother of God!"

Hovering on the edge of hysteria, I feigned laughter with them. But blood rose to color my cheeks, my knuckles whitened, and page eleven of *Dick and Jane* stuck to the palm of my hand. That's when I decided to hide my stuttering like Judy Cassidy who hid her purple birthmark under a sweater, even in summer.

This deception went on through all the elementary grades. In Grade 6, my refusal to participate in oral reading so enraged Mother St. George, who was as thin as a broomstick and couldn't take much pressure, that she demoted me to Grade 1 for two months. That afternoon, all thirty-four of my classmates, weeping copious crystal tears, led me the half block home in a solemn procession to defend me against the thwack of my mother's wooden spoon. For the next two months I squeezed my legs under the small desks and limped back to my own class in the afternoon to learn my sixth-grade lessons from Mother St. George.

By the time I got to university, I felt I was finally safe. Here, the professors did all the talking. But I hadn't counted on tradition and Mrs. Hollingsworth. In the second week, she stood behind the podium in our advanced English class and announced the annual public speaking contest that would account for half our first-term mark. All seventy-five students, most of whom I didn't know, would soon learn I stuttered. If I failed English, I'd lose my scholarship.

I lingered for a day on the shallow banks of indecision. Then a line from *Hamlet* I'd had to memorize came to me, '…if it be not now, yet it will come…' 'The readiness is all', Hamlet had said. Somehow these words gave me confidence. I began to prepare my eight-minute speech, polishing and buffing each and every word. I recited the speech so often, it began to haunt my dreams.

Then on October the twenty-first, when Mrs. Hollingsworth called my name, I rose from my desk and walked to the podium on wobbly legs, tripping on the only step I had to negotiate, but caught myself and my speech before both met up with the floor. With a tingling heart, I floated back to my seat. A girl elbowed me from behind with the news that I had won. Somehow I never even heard Mrs. H. announce my mark of ninety-eight percent.

My head dropped into my arms and I began to sob as classmates gathered around my desk. "Are you crying?" one of them asked.

"No," I mumbled, "I have an eyelash in my eye." When I finally sat up, I was shaking, but I smiled at all the kids around me. For the first time in my life, I was one of them.

Little did I know that within a few years, I'd be stepping in front of an audience five days a week as a teacher. In my first year of teaching, when the principal entered our students in the provincial public speaking contest, it didn't take me long to find Jonathan in my Grade ten English class. He looked away, slouching deeper in his seat, when I called for readers; he kept his head down, playing nervously with his hands, when I searched the class for answers. I asked him to meet with me at the end of the day.

"What did I do, Miss?" he asked, lumbering up to me, raising his head only to pose the question. "Nothing," I answered. "I have a proposition for you."

"Why would I enter a public speaking contest when I can barely read in class?" he moaned, shifting his weight from one foot to another.

"I'll work with you every day after school," I offered.

"I can't stay after class because I have to be home to watch over my brother," he protested, suddenly standing much straighter, relieved he'd found a good escape.

"No problem," I countered, "we'll work at your house." His shoulders sagged then and almost disappeared under his blue sweater.

For the next two and a half months he paced, he sweated every word, and he slapped his forehead when he stuttered. Sometimes, he'd sit in front of me and drop his head into his hands. But he never gave up. Slowly Jonathan's words began to take shape and sound. In early December, in a packed auditorium, Jonathan left my side and walked up to the podium wearing a suit he'd borrowed from his father that didn't quite fit. He didn't trip as I had. I watched Jonathan draw strength with every word. I felt a tear slide down my cheek as he bowed his head to receive the silver medal.

That summer I married and changed school boards. Now on a mission to help young students, I continued teaching public speaking after school.

Thirteen years later, as I lay in a hospital bed with a back injury, I was suddenly overwhelmed when a gang of my seniors stormed in and began serenading me with the school song. An intern appeared at my door to dispatch the raucous chorus. "Miss Kindellan!" the intern shouted from the doorway.

"Mrs. Sheehan," my horde corrected him. I couldn't see the intern above the maze of bobbing heads, but something in the catch of his voice caught my ear, a memory as clear as a crystal spring.

"All right guys," he shouted above the din, "Visiting hours are over." With the last jump and wave, their shoulders slung with knapsacks, my afternoon guests shuffled through the door. The fading sounds of their voices and footsteps receded as they moved down the hallway...

The intern walked slowly to the foot of my bed and whispered, "Do you remember me, Miss Kindellan?" I recognized the steady blue eyes of the intern smiling down at me, confident in his starched hospital whites. I recalled for a moment the seventeen-year-old student who'd shifted unsteadily on his feet in front of me, the shy kid who paced his basement while forcing a stubborn tongue to mouth his words, the scarecrow of a boy who walked to the podium in his father's suit and the devilish grin he flashed when he pretended to bite his silver medal.

"Don't cry, Miss,'" he whispered as he walked to the side of my bed. He leaned down then and kissed my cheek.

"How could I ever forget you, Jonathan?"

~ Sheila Kindellan-Sheehan

Honoring My Dreams

If you're Talented at music, that talent is of God. If something makes your heart sing, that's Gods way of telling you it's a contribution He wants you to make.
—Marianne Williamson

When I looked at myself in the mirror, the image I saw was of a frazzled woman in her thirties. I was too young to look like this, I thought. For a while, it seemed life had presented one crisis after another. As a wife and the mother of a three-year-old daughter, and a full-time job, my life had become so busy taking care of others I'd lost sight of my own dreams.

My husband, Robin, and I had been married almost eight years when we lost our second child, a boy. I'd been carrying him for almost five and a half months when the doctors discovered a serious problem. We were stunned to learn he had a heart defect, and that was coupled with Down Syndrome. When the doctor told us his chances of survival outside the womb were impossible, we were totally devastated.

The experience of saying goodbye to a son we would never get to know sent our lives into a tailspin. Like most parents, we had high hopes for our new baby. Now we were being told he had to leave us. Robin and I each struggled in our individual ways to cope with the sadness. While I cried a great deal, Robin held it in. Thankfully because of our ability to talk to each other about the loss of our unborn son, we managed to hold our marriage together. I loved my job, my work was fulfilling, and I felt I would manage to make it through.

Six months later almost to the day, the company I worked for went through a downsizing, my position was eliminated, and I was let go. I had been there for several years and loved the company. My feelings were understandably bruised.

I was still grieving the loss of my baby, and now had the loss of my job and the stress of unemployment to deal with. I became so drained and depressed I felt I might collapse from the mental and emotional strain.

Fortunately, I was able to find another job very quickly. However, although I was grateful for a source of steady income, the monotonous rut of going to work; preparing meals; folding laundry, and generally taking care of everyone except myself began to slowly erode my sense of self-worth and well being.

Back when I was a teenager, I'd had aspirations of becoming a singer. I absolutely loved to sing. But, when I learned that others considered me 'good, but not good enough,' I allowed the bitter truth of that message to sink in. Sadly, I gave up on my dream. When my friends who had enjoyed my singing, asked me to perform at parties, I started mumbling lame excuses. 'What was the point?' I reasoned silently. 'It wasn't going to get me anywhere'. For some reason, I no longer felt I had the *right* to sing, and stopped altogether.

A few years later, as I entered adulthood, I set my sights on a lucrative future in writing. I loved it, and knew I had a knack for it, so I set about attaining a degree. However, after a two-year college diploma in writing failed to produce a job in that field, I gave up on that dream as well. Needing to earn a living, I turned to the more attainable goal of becoming a secretary.

Now the lifestyle I had been living had drained my life force, and I felt a strong inner urge to make some changes. I've always known that dreams can reveal things about our deepest wishes. I began to have dreams where I was at a microphone belting out songs! The problem was, there was always a technical glitch. The power would short out, leaving me silent, and voiceless.

I realized my dream was telling me that my own power had been cut short. The way to gain it back would be to find an outlet for my voice – it was time to start singing again. I became determined to prove to myself that *I could be heard*. I knew in my heart this was that missing piece that once back in place, would bring joy and energy back into my life. I began to get excited!

I shared my dream with Robin and as always, he was very supportive. He understood and respected my creative leanings, and urged me to go for it. I went to a local music shop and put up an ad that said, "Singer Available." Then, went home, and held my breath.

Within the first week I began to get responses. The second call I got was from an established rock and country band looking for a singer to make things fresh again. I was excited when we all discovered I was just what they'd been looking for. After only one session singing with the band, I began to feel my enthusiasm for life returning.

Every Friday night I was at practice without fail. I found that the more I sang, the more my wounded self-esteem began to heal. I loved it so much, and found myself moving, thinking and *feeling* with a renewed sense of self.

I sang with that band for a wonderful two years. Then, when my second daughter was born, the demands on my time caused me to have to let it go once again. And, before long, I once again found the same feelings of spiritual lethargy creeping back in. Robin was working shift work, and arranging an evening out was difficult. I felt guilty for wanting time away from the children, and so once again, I put my needs on hold.

Pretty soon, just like before, my dreams began to communicate a need for a creative outlet. This time it was writing. My dreams were forcing me to realize that no matter what my personal obligations might be, my need for creative personal expression had to be honored, or I would pay the price.

When I found an online community magazine that was looking for articles, once again, I found a way to satisfy those creative urges. I was given my own column, and the thrill of seeing my articles published each week was wonderful.

These days, I fill the time with my commute to and from work with loud, joyous singing. My husband jokingly threatens to have the windows of our car tinted so other drivers don't think me wild. To ease his concerns, I recently placed another ad at the same local music store with the hopes of singing in a band once again.

I've heard many women my age lament about how with family demands, their creative aspirations seem to have slipped away. They wonder out loud what they might have become if they had chosen another path.

As it happens, I am not one of those women. I have learned that I don't have to put my dreams on the back burner, while my children grow up, in fact, it works better for everyone if I don't. Instead the energy I derive from self-fulfillment allows me to give back to my children, two-fold. I manage my treasured moments here and there to write my thoughts, and keep alive my creative spirit.

My dreams are what keep that sacred part of me alive. I never realized until recently how through living and fulfilling my own creative aspirations I am able to give my children the best I have to offer. And by showing them how to live their dreams and care for themselves emotionally and spiritually they will benefit for the rest of their lives.

~ *Brenda Chisholm*

God's Arm

A well has opened where my eyes were
Spiraling wind rushes through
Pushing past my memories,
Sweeping out the remnants of layers left over
There I am; holding on to God's arm
Reaching out with the other
Toward my life.
I let God move me,
Make my life
A motion of symmetry
A painting of graceful moments
Spent in Its arms.

~ *Darlene Montgomery*

Losing a Loved One

I will open my heart in trust that,

in ways I do not now understand,

my loved one will continue to be

present in my life.

— Martha Whitmore Hickman

Love Never Dies

It is by dying that one awakens to eternal life.
– Anonymous

On a Saturday morning in August, I was on my way to the post office when I took a wrong turn. Instead of turning left, I turned right and would have to double back through a series of turns.

As soon as I turned down the different route, I felt a silence everywhere. As I rounded a curve there in the middle of the road lay a man. My first thought was, '*He's a runner who's had a heart attack.*' I parked the car on the side of the road to see if I could help.

When I stepped out of the car, I felt as if I'd stepped into the presence of God. The area around the fallen man felt like a very holy place. Then I saw his terrible wounds and knew he'd been hit by a car and there wasn't much time.

I looked at him and said, "I'll be right back. May the blessings be." The latter is an ancient blessing in Eckankar.

I ran to the nearest house, yelling, "Call 911! Call for help!" They did. Then I ran back to the man and knelt beside him, singing HU, an ancient name for God.

The first notes came out as sobs, for my heart was breaking with compassion. I heard the Inner Master remind me, "Frances, you have a task to do. Focus on it." So I centered myself, and the HU came out as clear as a bell, "HU-U-U."

The man's body suddenly stopped spasming. He turned

and looked me in the eye. I knew Soul was recognizing the Light and Sound of God in the HU I sang. My inner hearing opened, and I could hear the man speaking. His only concern was for his family. 'My wife, my family,' he said silently, 'please let them know.'

I said to God, "How can I do this? This man doesn't have any identification on him."

The next minute, a man stopped his car and ran over. "Can I help?" he asked. Then as he knelt beside me, he gasped. "Oh, my God, it's Stan."

"Do you know this man?" I asked.

He nodded yes.

"Please, go get his family. He wants his family to know."

The man hurried away. The injured man relaxed as soon as he knew this was taken care of. His next concern was voiced to me silently: 'I need the blessings of God.'

I said aloud, "You have earned the right to walk in the presence of God. You have learned love and compassion and giving of yourself in this lifetime. You live forever in the worlds of God."

Soon the paramedics came and put the man in an ambulance. I continued to kneel at the side of the road, silently singing HU. A few minutes later, a small branch fell from a tree and landed gently beside me, and I felt waves of peace and love. I knew this Soul had translated from this world in the process we call death.

I left the scene sometime later, but for days I felt connected to this Soul. I was so touched by what had happened that I went to his funeral service. It confirmed everything that had been shown to me in those few precious moments in the middle of the road.

The minister spoke of how Stan had undergone a transformation in the last months of his life. He'd learned more about love and surrender and had a spiritual breakthrough while reading a particular story in the Bible.

The Bible story that touched him was about an angel

who had come to a man in the middle of the road. The angel wrestled the man to the ground, and the man asked, "Who are you?"

The angel said, "Why do you need to know?"

And the man in the story answered, "I need the blessings of God."

That story stuck my heart with love. After the service, I felt an urge to talk to Stan's wife, but I didn't want to overwhelm her with details of her husband's last moments. So I asked inwardly for help from Divine Spirit.

In that instant, someone called my name. It was a colleague of my husband's. He said, "Fran, I didn't know you knew Stan."

"I only met him in the last moments of his life," I said. "And the light around him was as bright as the morning sun."

"You've got to tell that to his wife," he said. "It will help her to hear your words." So he led me over and introduced me to Stan's wife; he mentioned I had found Stan and stayed with him in the road, and that I had an experience to share with her when the time was appropriate.

A few days later she called and invited me to come to her house. Stan's brother and some other relatives were there. She wanted me to tell them what had happened.

"I hope I can tell it without crying," I faltered.

"It's OK," she said. "We've all been crying."

When I finished sharing my story, the wife said, "I'm so grateful that you were there for my husband. He let me know too that he was well and in heaven. After the funeral I went to sit alone in our backyard, and a butterfly hovered around me. It wouldn't leave. In my church, a butterfly is a religious symbol of the resurrection."

"In my church," I said, "we believe Soul is eternal and lives forever." I felt she understood perfectly.

My experience with Stan's death was one of love and deep inner meaning, but I didn't know at the time that it was also one of preparation.

Just a few short weeks later, my own husband went into the hospital. Blackwell was an inspiration in his work as Jazz musician (a drummer), a composer, and teacher – and his perseverance with life, because for the past twenty years, he'd lived with kidney failure and was on dialysis. His colleagues said he was a walking miracle.

I didn't know this was to be his last stay in the hospital, but I knew I needed to be close to him. I had a cot put in his room. There were many poignant moments during this time. One night I found him quietly crying.

"I don't want to leave you," he said. "Do you know how much I love you?" Not long after that he went into intensive care.

It is never easy to let go of a loved one. But the transformation that took place on the roadside in early August eased my way. The doctors all tried to save my husband, but they knew they couldn't. I could see the unspoken words in their eyes. So I went to the hospital chapel and asked the *Mahanta, "Please show me beyond the shadow of a doubt what my husband wants."

My inner screen filled with brilliant blue, pulsating light. Then a golden light grew inside the field of blue. And my husband stood inside the light, happy and full of love.

"Tell me what you want," I asked.

"I'm ready to go," he said. "I love you."

I went back to the doctors. "There's something none of you have been able to say to me," I told them, "my husband is dying." We cried, and then we acknowledged that it was time to let go. I felt this set him free.

So we prepared for his leaving. His friends and family were there, and we had music from his latest recording playing in the room. He was surrounded by loved ones. In his final moments we all sang the HU. I saw the Mahanta take him into a heaven, one of the worlds of God. My heart was filled with gladness and sadness, both part of Divine Spirit, both part of divine love.

Darlene Montgomery

A few days later I was sitting on the edge of my bed crying. I missed my husband. Suddenly his presence filled the whole room and my heart with light and love.

He sang a song to me:

Don't cry for me.
Though I've gone away.
I'll never leave your heart.
I'll speak to you in the Voice of God.
Forever, you walk in my soul.
Don't cry for me,
Though I cherish your tears.
They are the way your heart can heal.
I'm never far.
And you're always near,
Between a smile and a tear.
Don't cry for me.
You know the beat goes on.
In the breath of all living things.
I'll sing life's song,
Sacred rhythm drum,
Beating time at its own game.
Don't cry for me –
I'm free.

A few weeks later, Laura, Stan's wife, sent me a card. In it she wrote that she had read about my husband's death and his courage. She said, "He was so fortunate to have you by his side."

I am grateful for the gifts these experiences have brought me. I'm discovering that love – all love – is God's love. And every act of giving with a loving heart brings us closer and closer to learning about a love for all life.

Celebrate life! Dare to love!
Love endures.
Love doesn't change.
Love lives forever.

~ *Frances Blackwell*

---

* Mahanta is the name for the Spiritual Guide for those on the path of ECKANKAR.

My Mother's Last Gift

All healing is essentially the release from fear.
— A Course in Miracles

My mother's name was Lillian, and she was the worst negative thinker in the world. Her life was very difficult. She grew up in a little border town between Poland and Lithuania, and when the Nazis came, they killed off the whole family. Other than she and her father, her whole family perished in the Holocaust.

That experience killed off my mother's faith. She often said, "If there is a loving God in the universe, then Holocausts don't happen, little babies don't die, and bad things don't happen to good people." She just sort of gave up. The way she dealt with her pain was to say, "I won't examine my life."

There were two things she taught me as a child. "Number one," she communicated clearly was, "Thou shalt not ever study psychology. If you get in touch with your pain, it will swallow you up." That was how she dealt with it, one foot after the other. The other thing she said was, "Whatever you do, don't study any religions other than Judaism." She didn't think there was anything interesting in Judaism anyway, but at least it was safe.

"Religion," she said, echoing Karl Marx, "is the opiate of the people. It is some kind of line you feed yourself to give meaning to an existence that's intrinsically meaningless." You'd think this kind of thinking would have killed her off quickly. But no, she lived to be 82, and that after a lifetime of smoking and drinking as well. This woman had cast-iron genes.

Lillian and I did not get along well. During the last year of her life, we had tried for months to talk about something with substance. I looked often at my relationship with my mother and father as part of my own healing. For years I had carried a great deal of anger about my mother. My chief definition of myself was not as "Joan," but rather, as "not Lillian." Whoever she was, I wanted to be different. That's about the most grievous form of attachment in non-forgiveness that I can think of. It kept me totally out of connecting with my own self, and with what my own life meant.

The healing for that has been a long road. But my mother's death in itself provided a remarkable healing as well.

The day she died, she had developed some internal bleeding. She was already in hospital, and at nine that morning they took her down to nuclear medicine for some tests. At four in the afternoon, she had not yet returned to her room, which by now was filled with her friends and relatives who had come to say goodbye. Concerned, they said, "Joan, she's going to die alone on a stretcher somewhere out there unless you go get her." So, I put on my white coat, and resolutely made my way to nuclear medicine. When I found her, she was lying there all alone on a stretcher. She had been there all day. Something had happened. There had been an accident, an emergency, so they let her wait.

I was very upset. Under these circumstances, you really have to assert yourself. Don't let them take your loved ones away without a second thought. I looked at the doctor and said, "This won't do. We have to have her back." And the doctor replied, "I'm sorry, we need a diagnosis."

My mother, always the joker said, "Aahhh! That's why I've been lying here all day? Why didn't you ask me?"

The startled doctor said, "What?"

And my mother replied, "I'm dying. There's your diagnosis."

And so I got her out of there. To return her to her room,

they needed to put her in an elevator only large enough for the stretcher and one other person, the orderly. So the orderly said, "You'll have to meet her in her room."

"No," I said, "I don't," and then I kicked him out of the elevator. This is against hospital rules. You're not allowed to wheel your own family member around. God forbid, something could happen.

Alone in the elevator, she looked at me, knowing this might be our last chance ever to say anything. "Joan, I have to complete this with you," she said. "I know I've made a lot of mistakes. I know it and I'm sorry. Can you forgive me?"

Hearing those words was wonderful. But even more wonderful was that I now had the chance to acknowledge all the mistakes I had made, not by making a list, but just by feeling the feeling. My mother was not interested in long emotional lists. That wasn't her style.

But I did have a list. I was sorry we had never been friends; that I couldn't be there for her as often as I would have liked to; that I had held her in judgment, and most of all I was sorry I had kept her out of my heart. But, just being able to look her in the eyes and say, "Can you forgive me for the mistakes I have made?"

And having her say, "Yes," provided the healing of a lifetime. It was truly amazing.

When I got her back to the room, everyone had gone for a cup of coffee. With the short time left, I looked at her and said, "How about we exchange soul qualities?" Now, this was not the sort of woman with whom one exchanged soul qualities, but in this great moment of openness she said, "Oh sure, I'd love to."

And so I began; "What I've always admired about you was your courage and that you've had a tremendous fortitude no matter what." I tend to crumble when the going gets tough.

She said, "I'll give you that." Then she said, "What I would like from you is compassion." The fact that she could even see that in me, that I could be compassionate to everybody else but her, was most amazing.

Some hours later, my twenty-year-old son Justin had arrived. He was very close to his grandparents. Over the years he had spent a lot of time with my mother, she often babysat him when he was little.

Most of that night, he lay in bed and held her. We said prayers to her and sang everything you could think of. Finally, about three in the morning, she was asleep. Justin and I were sitting on opposite sides of the bed, and I was meditating. It was then I had the vision.

I have had only one vision. It was definitely not a dream. It was very different from a dream. All I can say is it was much more real than this level of reality. The old Tibetans say that we are dreaming now. This life is the substance of a dream. When we leave this life, is when we actually wake up.

In this vision, I was a pregnant woman, giving birth to a baby. My consciousness was somehow present in both places. I was both the pregnant mother and the baby.

Then I was a baby being born experiencing a terrible dark night of the soul. I was dying. I was dying to the world of the womb, being born to a whole new life. I was being born, coming through the birth canal and out of the darkness, into the most resplendent light. In that moment of birth, I suddenly knew everything about my relationship with my mother, all knowledge, right there.

When I opened my eyes, the room was filled with light. There were no barriers between things. Everything was energy, everything was light. Everything was interpenetrating with everything else. I looked across the bed and Justin was weeping, the tears pouring down his face. His face was luminous, like he had seen the face of God.

"The room is filled with light," he whispered. "Can you see it?"

"Yes," I replied.

"It's Grandma's last gift," he said. "She's holding open the door to eternity so we can have a glimpse."

He looked at me with such tenderness, and said, "You must feel so grateful to her." I realized then he had had a vision, too, and that I *was* grateful. He said, "You know, she was a very great soul. She had tremendous wisdom. She came and took a role much smaller than the wisdom she had, in order to give you something to resist so you could become who you are. Isn't there a word for that?"

The word he was looking for was Boddhisatva, from the Buddhist tradition. I think we are all Boddhisatvas in a way, in that we don't come for ourselves alone. We come because we grow as a group. We grow through what we share with other people. We grow through difficulties, perhaps more than we grow through the times when things go well. We are part of a greater holy and sacred mystery.

Here is the most important thing for you to keep in mind: You are never alone. If you could see, there are more beings of light here sustaining you than there are people in flesh bodies. You are never alone. Any attempt you make to become quiet inside, to pray, to bring forth a light for yourself makes a difference in this universe. As each one of us heals, we never heal alone. Our own healing always uplifts the whole of which we are a part.

~ Joan Borysenko, Ph.D.

To See My Skye Again

There is no death! What seems so is transition;
This life of mortal breath
Is but a suburb of the life elysian,
Whose portal we call Death.
— Henry Wadsworth Longfellow

After my beautiful eight-year-old daughter Skye died of Leukemia in 1968, I felt such a great loss. In Skye's short time with me, we had traveled the world together, lived in Australia and New Zealand, and on our last trip traveled on board a cruise liner to Egypt where we had an incredible time.

She and I were both highly intuitive and had the ability to see beings from other planes who walk on earth, so we shared something most mothers and daughters don't. We were very close.

We'd moved back to England two years before the tragedy. Shortly afterward, Skye developed fluelike symptoms which turned out to be Leukemia. After my sweet Skye died, when I did sleep, I had a recurring dream in which I would be standing before a very large grey, early Georgian style house. Entering the house, I was always confronted by the same endless white corridors. In each dream the scene was replayed with me searching in absolute desperation to find Skye.

Occasionally I would meet what looked like a nurse or a doctor and would ask where Skye was. I would be pointed down one way or another and off I would go driven by the urgency of Skye needing me and knowing she was alone in her illness.

This terrible and haunting dream persisted for many months until one night it took a different turn. This time I entered the house as usual and followed the many corridors – where I was finally directed to go upstairs. I had never been upstairs before, and didn't know there was an upstairs.

There I found myself in what appeared to be a very large old-fashioned theatre sitting up in the gallery overlooking an immense stage. In the dim light I saw a line of children on the stage, singing. My eyes moved down the line and then I saw her. It was Skye on the end of the line, wearing her favorite sweater! Our eyes met in a moment of recognition. The love between us acted as a magnet, lifting both of us up and drawing us together. We exploded together in warmth and joy in mid air!

A feeling of wonderful warmth and delight surrounded me as I awoke. I had finally found my beloved daughter!

Many dreams followed where Skye would show up in shops, on streets or on buses. Skye always took my hand assuring me she was well and happy.

My Grandmother passed away in 1989. She and I had had a very close relationship. I had lived with her on and off in the war years. She had been like a second mother to me. When I was back in England in 1988 she told me she really wanted to die. She was 93 and many friends and most family were gone. She was frail and tired easily.

She wasn't afraid to die, and was quite psychic so we chatted about it, and I said to her, "Grandma, if you die please try and reach me if you can. Let me know how you are."

A few weeks after she died Grandma appeared to me in a dream.

Her appearance was now of a 45 year old with hair curly and bobbed and she was dressed all in purple, with a long string of purple beads. The bizarre part was that she was riding an immense motorbike that looked like a Norton – and she was laughing and telling me it was wonderful. The dream was very real and I awoke from it feeling happy and jubilant.

I had the same dream some nights later – Grandma riding into my bedroom on this immense motorbike, dressed in purple, looking younger – and saying to me, "Look who I found."

Sitting perched behind her, blonde hair blowing as if in wind, was Skye. They were both laughing and happy and drove off through the wall.

I haven't had many dreams of them since that night. My dream was a true gift from heaven that has helped to heal the pain I felt at their loss. Since then I've remarried and had another beautiful daughter that I named Skye. There are remarkable similarities between her and my Skye of those many years back. I always knew I'd see Skye again. I know that life continues and that real healing comes through knowing our loved ones live on even beyond this life.

~ *Patricia Orwin*

He Sendeth Sun, He Sendeth Shower

He sendeth sun, he sendeth shower,
Alike they're needful for the flower:
And joys and tears alike are sent
To give the soul fit nourishment.
As comes to me or cloud or sun,
Father! thy will, not mine be done
Oh, ne'er will I at life repine:
Enough that thou hast made it mine.
When falls the shadow cold of death
I yet will sing, with parting breath,
As comes to me or shade or sun,
Father! thy will, not mine, be done!

~ Sarah Flower Adams

The Spirit of a Child

It was a Friday night in March. My teenage son Ryan and I were standing on our front porch. He was wearing his usual teenage uniform – baggy jeans, oversized T-shirt and baseball cap. I was trying to convince him he needed a jacket, but the unseasonably warm temperatures had him insisting otherwise. He was heading out to meet friends at a local Tim Hortons and was determined he didn't need a coat. I was determined he did.

I'd always hated the thought of him being cold, and now that he was a teenager it was even more of a challenge to get him to dress sensibly. He finally relented and put on his oversized navy Wind River sweatshirt. I kissed him on his cheek, the way I'd done a million times before, and watched as he headed down the driveway. He looked back at me and smiled the way he always did, half embarrassed, half liking it.

"Home by midnight," I said, as I waved goodbye. That would be the last time I'd see him or kiss him on his cheek again. It was around midnight when I awoke to a knock. I rushed downstairs, figuring Ryan forgot his keys. Instead, I made out the shadowy but unmistakable figures of two police officers. My stomach clenched. I took a deep breath and opened the door.

"Do you have a son named Ryan?" one of them asked. I let them in. We sat down. They looked uncomfortable and exchanged uneasy glances. Then, one began to talk. A large group of teens had gathered for a bush party at a local soccer park. There'd been a lot of alcohol. Around 11 p.m., one boy wandered over to the railway tracks and fell into the path of an eastbound freight train. I felt sick. I knew where they were going with the story. I'd heard it before when I covered the police beat as a reporter. But in my world, those tragedies only happened to other people. The officer listed items they found at the scene: maroon watchband, jeans, baseball cap. "Yes," I said, "but that could be anyone." "Did he have braces?" asked the officer. "He had a wire retainer." "Did he have an asthma inhaler in his pocket?" A chill went through me. "I think I better call my father," I said, jumping up.

My father lived a block away. He arrived in minutes. I still remember how he almost collapsed when the officers told him they had reason to believe Ryan had been killed. He kept shouting, "No, no, no." I was angry at him for believing them so readily and ran upstairs to find Ryan's dental X-rays and the fingerprints from the Child Find booklet. I gave them to the officers and they headed out the door to the hospital. I knew once they checked them, they'd realize they'd made a terrible mistake. The officers left. My father phoned my mother and gave her the news. We sat in the living room numb and mostly in silence. Part of me knew the officers were right. My son was dead and I'd never see him again, but I couldn't accept it. I went into a state of shock that stayed with me for days.

During those days there was so much to do – all the funeral arrangements, writing the obituary, picking out a burial plot. I was in such a bewildered state and wanted to do everything right for my son, while at the same time I still didn't believe he was gone. I remember walking through the rows of coffins thinking, how do you choose a coffin for your only child?

I got through those early days by putting one foot in front of the other and by relying on every survival strategy I'd ever learned in life. I was floating on a cushion of shock, still clinging to the possibility a mistake had been made. How could my son, who had been the centre of my life for almost 19 years, suddenly be gone? It was unimaginable. My life and

Ryan's had been a single braid. I'd raised him on my own since he was six months old. His father and I had separated and there were no visiting rights. I'd watched him sprout from a three-and-a-half-pound premature infant into a handsome six-foot-three-inch young man with size 12 feet.

For more than 18 years, our lives were wrapped around each other in a relationship unique to single parents. We'd been through the colicky nights, the emergency ward visits for his asthma attacks, the teacher interviews, the trip to Tokyo where he entertained the Japanese during our rides on the subways and our famous wrestling matches. We'd always wrestled, leaving the house looking like a hurricane zone.

Living with Ryan, I would joke with him, was like living with Kato from the Peter Sellers movies in which he played Inspector Clouseau. When he wasn't jumping out of closets at me, he was charging at me from across the room. We'd end up in one of our wrestling matches that always finished with us laughing till we cried.

Ryan had a definite gift for making people laugh. Friends were important to him and he valued them more than anything. He took time to be with people and friends told me he always knew the right thing to say when someone was down. As a result, he had a wealth of friends. For many of those friends, our home was their second home and it was often filled with the voices of teenagers, their video games and their music. They'd visit after school and on weekends and empty my fridge of chicken nuggets and plum sauce. They'd sleep on the couch and family room floor and rise late the next day to play more video games. At times I wished they'd find another spot, but at the same time I loved it that they felt comfortable in our home. After all, I always knew where Ryan was.

It was spring and Ryan was preparing for a new chapter in his life. He was to head off to college to study broadcast journalism in September. Now, suddenly, he was gone. In one second, I lost my son and the right to call myself a mother.

The teenage laughter in the house was gone, as was the sound of video games. For the first few weeks, none of it seemed real. But as the weeks wore on, the reality began to sink in and so began my journey into grief. I became more and more incapacitated to the point where I couldn't eat or sleep or concentrate on anything for more than a few seconds. I was exhausted and running on empty. To make matters worse, I took up smoking after finding an old pack of cigarettes in Ryan's room. I hadn't smoked since high school, but within a week I was smoking a pack a day.

Friends and family became my lifelines. They brought me casseroles and homemade soups, scented candles and healthy salads. They drove me to the cemetery and stayed with me through the night. People I'd never met, but who knew me from my work at The Hamilton Spectator, reached out with cards and letters. Each act of kindness helped me get through another minute.

Ryan's friends visited by the dozens and became my most precious lifelines. I'd sit with them and reminisce about the funny things Ryan did. Teenagers were so much more honest with their grief than adults. They'd laugh and cry and hold each other when they needed someone to hang on to. They loved my son dearly, and their emotional honesty was a refreshing reminder to me of how special he was. His friends made up many of the 400 people who came to the funeral. They were from high schools all over Burlington and cut across all lines. Boys and girls, young and old. Ryan was like that. No boundaries, no rules, as long as they knew how to laugh.

I was fortunate in that my supervisors at The Spectator never pressured me to return to work. In fact, quite the opposite. They insisted I take the time I needed to heal, paid for a yoga instructor to come to my home to teach me stress-reduction exercises and even covered the cost of a Chinese dinner on my first Mother's Day.

I counted on my friends to get me through each day, especially as the pain deepened. But while many encircled me with caring, there were others who added to my pain. They'd visit, then say cruel, hurtful things or ramble on about their own problems. Others, some of whom I considered my closest friends, disappeared without a trace. I tried to understand their absence. I knew I wasn't easy to be with, but I was too disabled with grief to teach anyone how to be with me. I learned later this was a common experience among bereaved parents.

"Losing your child is the true litmus test of a friendship," one bereaved parent told me.

Those people who stuck by me taught me about the true meaning of friendship, but even my best friends had to go home sometime. And when they did, a horrible silence came over the house. All those things I'd taken for granted were gone – his voice on the phone, his laughter, the shuffling of his baggy jeans when he walked down the hall, the smell of his Old Spice deodorant, the constant beep-beep of his video games.

There were times when I felt like I was literally on fire. Sometimes I felt panicky and out of control. I was coping one minute and the next I couldn't breathe. I would hyperventilate and run from room to room, unable to catch my breath. Grief, I learned, was extremely physical. The pain was so intense, I felt like I'd come off an anesthetic halfway through an operation, while still cut open and bleeding. I couldn't handle loud noises, even the sound of windshield wipers. Watching TV was impossible because of the constant images of violence. And every song on the radio reminded me of Ryan. It seemed every time I went into a store, I heard LeeAnn Rimes singing "How Do I Live Without You". Even carrying on a conversation became difficult. I'd forget simple words, fumble about like a stroke victim then give up.

Before the accident I juggled a demanding career, single parenthood and caring for my home. Now making a cup of tea was an effort. I was proud of my photographic memory, which served me well as a reporter. Now, there were times I couldn't remember my own phone number. Many times I felt helpless and ready to give up but another part of me, the fighter, was determined to make it through. I was exhausting my friends and knew I needed to reach out for help. I started reading bereavement books but found them too clinical and began searching for a bereavement counselor. I knew from my research as a reporter that the counselling business is problematic. Anyone can hang up a shingle and call themselves a counselor, so it's buyer beware.

Most counselors I met were kind and gentle hand-holder types but knew little about the process of grieving or, more important, how to help me heal and move forward. Then I met Lori and Tony Antidormi. Their two-and-a-half-year-old son Zachary had been stabbed to death by a neighbor. The date of Zachary's death was March 27, 1997, exactly one year before Ryan died. The couple had not only survived the loss of their only child, but the pain of a high profile court case and subsequent inquest. Lori wrote to me and offered her support and I gladly accepted. She and Tony helped me understand that time does heal wounds and assured me I would someday feel my spirit again. I found hope, not only in their words, but in seeing people who had rebuilt their lives and found new joy. We kept in touch, visiting and phoning.

About a year and a half after my son died, I experienced a dramatic turning point. I woke up one morning and felt a lightness so acute it was like I'd come out of a tunnel. I believe I simply bottomed out on grief. I'd indulged in it, talked it out, acted it out, smoked my brains out. It was time to come back. Although I still weathered my share of ups and downs, I was moving forward. I eased back into work, set up a fitness routine and eventually quit smoking. Most important, I moved forward on plans to become a mother again.

Within months of losing my son, I'd thought about adopting a child. I'd tasted the joys of parenthood and knew nothing was better. I missed those things that make parenting so magical – waking up to my son's laughter, teaching him to ride a bike, seeing his face on Christmas morning. And I missed being part of something bigger than my own little world.

Since the moment Ryan came into my life, I'd felt part of some universal community, one in which we were connected by a greater purpose, that of being a parent. Someone had mentioned the idea of adopting from China and advised me to look into it, partly because China allows single people to adopt and also because the children are fairly healthy and the adoption process is smooth. I'd already met with a social worker and begun the paperwork to adopt a little Chinese girl. I'd also signed on with Open Arms to International Adoption to facilitate the adoption and received approval from the Ontario ministry of community, family and children's services.

Now it was time to take the most important leap – ask them to send my application to China. I faltered. I didn't know if I could handle being a parent again. I questioned whether my heart would ever heal enough for me to fully give my love to another child. A close friend who adopted three children and who stuck by me gave me the best advice of anyone.

"Just keep moving ahead," he said. "If it feels wrong when you get on that plane, you can always change your mind."

It was good advice. I moved ahead. On June 13, 2000, one day after my son's birthday, I received a phone call from Open Arms director Deborah Maw saying she had five photos and medical reports for a nine-month-old baby girl named Ling Zhu. "She's absolutely beautiful," said Deborah. I tore into Toronto, bursting with anticipation. Deborah opened a file folder to reveal five photos of the little girl who was to be my daughter. I gasped. She had a beautiful moon-shaped angel face, rosebud lips, a soft fringe of dark hair. Her eyes held such intelligence, her sweet mouth held such promise. I couldn't wait to hold her but at the same time, I was panic-stricken over whether I could give this beautiful child the life she deserved. There were still times when I felt crippled with grief. I decided to heed my friend's advice and keep moving ahead.

Two months later, I boarded a plane with a friend and five other couples who also worked through Open Arms and we made the grueling trip to the other side of the world. After two long days of sitting in planes and airports, we arrived at the Novotel Hotel in the city of Hefei, province of Anhui. It was midnight and there was little time to recover. At 9 o'clock the next morning, we met in a conference room in the hotel. A few minutes later, a line of Chinese nannies walked into the room, each carrying a nine-month-old baby wearing identical blue sleepers. I searched the little girls' faces to see if I could find my daughter.

A few minutes later, someone called out, "Ling Zhu." I rushed forward. Her nanny placed her in my arms. Her hair was pulled tightly into yellow butterfly clips so she didn't look like her pictures. She felt small and stiff and not at all comfortable with this new person. I stroked her face and told her I was her forever mommy and that she would be coming to live with me in a country called Canada. An hour later, she fell asleep in my arms and I started to fall in love. By the next day, it was clear she'd decided our partnership was going to work. She clung to me with a certainty that convinced me we were absolutely meant to be together. A few days after our meeting, she looked at me and said, "Momma." That sealed our union.

I named her Emma, which appropriately means universal healer, and kept her Chinese name Ling as her middle name to honor her heritage. Ling Zhu means bright pearl, which she most certainly is. There's a light around this child of mine that lights up a room like 100 fireflies. I'll never meet the Chinese official who matched us, but they clearly saw something in our eyes and knew we were meant to be together. Sometimes she seems wise beyond her years, perhaps because her journey here was a long one, as was mine. I'll probably never meet her Chinese mother who was forced to give her up because of the government's one-child policy. But I think about her often. Maybe that's because I know the pain of losing a child. I wish I could scream out to her that her little girl is beautiful and healthy and safe and, most of all, that she is loved. I don't know if it would fill the pain of not having her in her arms.

Some people believe losing my son was part of a divine plan that led me to China to adopt my little girl. The randomness of such a tragedy is just too terrifying. They believe there must be some reason. The sad truth is, there's never a reason for losing a child. Ryan was taken from this world too soon and a great many things were left undone in his passing. He'll never meet his little sister but he did play a part in her becoming my daughter. He taught me about the joys of motherhood. Now my daughter is continuing his lessons. I've told my daughter about her big brother and his beautiful smile, piercing blue eyes and witty humor. When she's older, I'll tell her how much he loved roller coasters and chicken nuggets and video games. I'll tell her how much he loved his friends and how much they loved him back. I'll keep his spirit alive so he can teach his sister about life. That's what big brothers are for.

~ *Denise Davy*

Bathroom Humor

The best way to find yourself is to lose yourself
in the service of others.
— Gandhi

Dad taught me not to be afraid to try something new. If I did and failed, he was there to help me pick up the pieces. He taught me to stand up to authority with courage, wit, wisdom and knowledge; always keep my sense of humor and photocopy everything; to be kind to people whom are down and out.

On one occasion while on vacation, Dad saw an older gentleman at the side of the road. The man looked down and out, with scruffy appearance and ratty clothes. Dad stopped the car and said, "Sorry buddy, we don't have room to give you a ride." But Dad opened the trunk, pulled a pair of his pants out of a suitcase and gave them to the man.

The best lesson of all from my father is that humor should underline all of life's up and downs. Even when Dad was in his final hours in the hospital, with family and friends gathered around him, he kept up with the funny lines. My sister, Donna was trying to get ice chips in his mouth to quench his thirst. Dad piped up, "Oh sure, you will give me ice chips, but can I have a cigarette?" We later sewed a pack of smokes into his pant pocket before the funeral director came to take him away.

On his final day, Dad was unable to speak. But I was able to communicate with him through his eyebrows. We worked out a system where I would ask questions and he would signal me by moving his eyebrows up and down: once for 'no', twice for 'yes' and three or four times if he was showing me he was laughing.

It was amazing. He confirmed for me three times that day that he was ready to go. He saw a white light and felt at peace. Near the final hours, I said, "Hey Dad, when you get where you are going, give us a sign, okay?"

Mom was sitting on the other side of his bed and said, "Yeah Ed, surprise Heather in the shower. Turn the lights off and on while she is having a shower!" I saw Dad's expression for laughter with those eyebrows and said, "No way Dad, no bathroom humor, that's not very funny." He moved his eyebrows to show us his laughter.

It was later that evening around ten minutes to eleven with family and friends at his side that he left us peacefully. The decibel level in the room had skyrocketed as we laughed, told jokes and reminisced. As Dad slipped away, we all felt euphoric knowing he was finally at peace. He left with a warm smile on his face. We were certain that the laughter and chatter had made him feel the comfort of home.

The next morning around quarter to seven, I heard Mom leaving the upstairs bathroom after having her shower. I entered the bathroom next. When I was done showering, I pulled back the curtain and reached for a towel on the vanity. All of a sudden, four tiles from around the back of the tub starting flying off the wall. One smashed on the edge of the tub. It was almost as if someone had a chisel and was prying them one by one in an orderly fashion.

I knew at that moment it was my dad but I was not afraid as a calm, warm, peaceful feeling swept over me. I screamed, laughed and cried all at the same time.

I could not get dried and dressed fast enough. I pulled Mom into the bathroom and showed her the missing tiles yelling, "He was here! It was Dad and he got there okay, he really is okay and that was the sign!" We hugged, laughed and shared the moment as we stormed into my brother Brent's room to re-cap. We then realized that not only had Dad installed those tiles himself some twenty years earlier, but he had also said he never really liked them!

Later that morning, I was walking through the kitchen past my brother-in-law Tom, who was standing beside Brent seated at the table. Dad was there, not far from the door by his favorite chair. He was there for a brief moment. I froze and said; "Did you guys see that? Dad was here!"

They looked at me rather strangely and said, "No."

I said, "Gee, why is Dad choosing me?"

Donna looked up and said with a grin, "Cause, you kept yacking at him in the hospital and would not shut up!"

I could almost hear Dad laughing off in the distance in total agreement.

~ *Heather Thompson*

Gifts from a Dying Sister

I believe that imagination is stronger than knowledge
That myth is more potent than history
That dreams are more powerful than facts
That hope always triumphs over experience
That laughter is the only cure for grief
And I believe that love is stronger than death.
– Robert Fulgham

When we were children, my sister Josie and I were very close. The elder by two years, I was the extrovert, the leader, the fearless one.

My parents used to say, "Because you are the eldest, you have to care for your little sister."

Josie followed me around while I created all kinds of situations for both of us to experience. It was the way things were in those days. We both seemed to accept each other's roles. This was our relationship and it continued more or less the same way until she was twenty-four. At that point Josie married a man eight years her senior and moved to another city. From then on, our relationship changed dramatically. Our lives moved in different and very separate directions.

Then, at age 40, Josie became ill with lung cancer. She moved back to Toronto and our lives reconnected on a journey that lasted eighteen months.

It was during this ordeal that for the first time in many years we told one another how much we cared for and loved each other. Josie said to me: "I don't want to die." I told her that I didn't want her to die and promised to care for her two children if she did not recover. We were beginning to bond again in love, as sisters.

One evening during a session with a healing professional, Josie revealed how much she had envied and resented me when we were children. She confessed that she had always wanted to be like me. This secret had been locked in her mind and heart all these years. I could see how painful it was to open up, communicate, and share her innermost feelings. I never really knew my sister until the end of her life. Only then did I glimpse Josie's strength, power and beauty.

Finally we connected on a soul level. No words were necessary. She revealed herself quietly just by being there. At the end of her life, my little sister gave me two of the greatest gifts that I will ever have, those of knowing eternal life and divine love.

Death had always been a remote concept for me. I'd had no reason to think of it as no one close to me had ever died. I always felt I understood death, both intellectually and spiritually but with Josie's illness, I faced one of life's greatest mysteries. I discovered my resistance, my ignorance, my deep fear of death and the pain associated with it.

The reality that my sister would soon die crept closer. I could not escape it, even though there were many times when I just wanted to close my eyes and sink into oblivion. The pain I experienced every time I looked at the almost skeletal figure of my beloved sister was unbearable.

Near the end of her life Josie weighed only 70 lbs. and became blind in one eye. I wanted desperately to take away the emotional and psychological pain she was experiencing, and protect her from the humiliation she felt from the unwanted stares of people whenever we took her home from the hospital on a day pass. Whenever our eyes locked, I could read her question: "Why is this happening to me?" I could give her no reason, no meaning, no answers.

Every minute of every day, the reality of her death was coming closer and closer. I began to feel anger at her indirectly for forcing me to go through this experience, one I felt I had not chosen.

One night, several months before Josie died, I consciously allowed myself to imagine what her moment of death would be like. At first I was terrified, especially because when imagining her dying in a cold hospital room, instead of the warmth of home. At first it was overwhelming, but then an awareness and calm came over me. I asked for spiritual guidance and another way to experience her death without fear. I started to breathe slowly, relax, and focus in the energy field of source within me. Images began to form of Josie and me as children. I imagined how I would feel and what I would say to her.

I saw a scene of what the last moments of her dying would be like. At the end of my meditation, I felt uplifted and peaceful. I knew then that I would be by her side when the time came for Josie to leave this physical world.

Months later, on a Sunday afternoon in a hospital room, my sister was leaving. I knew it. I was there, as well as her children and our mother. Our father and brother came later. I could feel soul slowly and gently leaving her body. Her daughters held her by one hand and I the other, while stroking her hair. I felt such intense love for Josie and I knew she felt it as well. It was as if my heart (I could feel this as a physical sensation in the center of my chest area) was breaking open to stretch beyond its normal capacity.

All the time, her soul slowly began to depart her body, I whispered words of love, support, reassurance, and guidance towards the Light. I experienced being totally connected to Josie and my Spiritual Source. I felt at peace, for I knew where she was going.

The truth was coming from a place deep within me and I had a knowing beyond anything my mind could have imagined. I did not actually see any particular light, but felt a strong energy field of peace and love encompassing the two of us. It was coming from inside us, permeating the whole room. As her life force left her body, I felt Josie slowly emerging to the other side.

My dearest, beautiful sister was peacefully surrendering her body while her soul came closer and closer to spirit. In the last minutes of her dying, there were no barriers, no separation. I could feel only Spirit, hers and mine, were one. It was the same energy, the same substance. Through her death, I experienced life, the living Spirit and the vibration of love, more intensely and deeply than I had ever experienced before in my life. The mystery of death had finally revealed itself to me.

Through her death, my sister gave me the greatest of gifts. I now know that death is an aspect of the continuum of life, and the end of a cycle. It is the final surrender of our body and our ego to love and spirit. The beauty, the power, and the peace this gift contains has enriched my life and has transformed me beyond the measure.

I miss you dearest sister, and when I think of your body, that empty shell beneath the earth, I feel an ache in the center of my chest, an ache so deep. If I close my eyes, however, and go within and feel our love, I know you are safe and well and this brings me peace.

~ *Medea Bavarella Chechik*

Do Not Stand at My Grave and Weep

Do not stand at my grave and weep
I am not there. I do not sleep.
I am a thousand winds that blow.
I am the diamond glints on snow.
I am the sunlight on ripened grain.
I am the gentle autumn rain.
When you awaken in the morning's hush
I am the swift uplifting rush
Of quiet birds in circled flight.
I am the soft stars that shine at night.
Do not stand at my grave and cry;
I am not there. I did not die.

– Mary Elizabeth Frye

Ryan's Hope

... Weeping may remain for a night,
but rejoicing comes in the morning.
- Psalm 30:5

The day started out normally enough. It was May 1, 1997. Ryan was upstairs preparing to leave for school, while his six-year-old sister, Jamie, waited for him at the front door. Suddenly Ryan started to tell us about Albert Einstein with such enthusiasm and excitement, it was as if a light had gone off in his head. He said, "$E=mc^2$ – I understand what Einstein was saying: the theory of relativity. I understand now!"

I said, "That's wonderful," but thought, *How odd.* It wasn't his thinking about Einstein – Ryan was so intelligent – but rather the timing that seemed peculiar.

At ten years old, Ryan loved knowledge and seemed to have an abundance of it, far beyond his years. The possibilities of the universe were boundless to him. When he was in first grade, the children in his class were asked to draw a picture and answer the question, 'If you could be anyone, who would you be?' Ryan wrote: "If I could be anyone, I'd want to be God." At age seven, while sitting in church one day, he wrote.

The tree of Life, O, the tree of Glory,
The tree of God of the World O, the tree of me.

Somehow I think Ryan just "got it."

In the midst of his strange outburst about Einstein, Ryan suddenly called out that he had a headache. I went upstairs and found him lying on his bed. He looked at me and said, "Oh, Mommy, my head hurts so bad. I don't know what's happening to me. You've got to get me to the hospital."

By the time we arrived at the hospital in Newmarket he was unconscious. We stood by helplessly as the doctors fought to save his life, and then they transferred him by ambulance to Toronto's Hospital for Sick Children.

A couple of hours later we were finally allowed to see him. He was hooked up to a life support system. When the doctor told us our son had suffered a massive cerebral hemorrhage and was "legally and clinically brain dead." It felt like a nightmare. We went into shock. Nothing more could be done, the doctor said, and asked if we would consider organ donation. Astonishingly, we had discussed this with Ryan only recently. We looked at each other and simultaneously replied, "Oh yes, Ryan would have wanted that."

In April, Ryan had seen his dad filling out the organ donor card on the back of his driver's license. His dad had explained to him about organ donations and how you could help save another's life by agreeing to donate your organs when you die. When Ryan wondered if you needed a driver's license to do this, his dad replied that anyone could donate their organs.

Organ donations made such perfect sense to Ryan, he went on his own campaign persuading the entire family to sign donor cards. We had no doubt that donating Ryan's organs was the right thing to do.

After a small bedside service, we said our good-byes to our son. When we left the hospital, we left a part of ourselves behind. Driving home, I could feel a thick fog roll in and surround me, crushing me. We were in total disbelief. My husband Dale, and I cried in each other's arms all that night and for many nights after. It was as if part of me had died with my son.

Grief consumed me for a long time. We kept waiting for Ryan to walk in the door. We grieved for the loss of today, and also for the loss of our hopes and dreams. I realize now you never get over the death of your child. With time you heal, but you are forever changed. It was our daughter Jamie who gave us a reason to get up in the morning and carry on.

Then on a beautiful morning four months after Ryan's death, the first letter arrived, addressed to my husband and me, As we read it, we both began to weep. It was from a twenty-year-old university student thanking us for our "gift of sight." He had received one of Ryan's corneas and could now see again. It is difficult to describe our emotions – we wept, but at the same time, we felt wonderful.

Sometime later, we received a second letter from a young woman of thirty who had received one of Ryan's kidneys and his pancreas. She told us that because of Ryan, she was now free from insulin and dialysis, able to work again and return to normal life.

Early May brought the painful first anniversary of our son's death. Then we received our third letter. A young boy of sixteen, born with cystic fibrosis, had received Ryan's lungs. Without the double lung transplant he received, he would have died. Besides being able to return to school, he was now doing things he had never done before – running, playing hockey and roller blading with his friends. Knowing this boy's life had been renewed lifted our spirits immensely.

Due to confidentiality laws, organ donation is completely anonymous in Canada. However, organ recipients and their donor families can communicate through the organ transplant organization. Although we did not know the identities of the individuals who had received Ryan's organs, we were given updates about their health.

We learned about a six-year-old girl who had received Ryan's other kidney and was now healthy, free from dialysis and attending school full time. We also learned that the forty-two-year-old woman who had received Ryan's liver was doing well and was able to again spend time with her young family.

Such joy seemed to come from your sorrow, so much happiness from our loss.

Although nothing could take away our pain, we took great comfort and peace in knowing that Ryan had done something most of us will never do – he had saved lives!

That summer while on vacation in Haliburton, we met a young man – by sheer coincidence – who had had a kidney and pancreas transplant at the same hospital where some of Ryan's organs had been transplanted. He knew the young woman who had received her kidney and pancreas on May 2 from a ten-year-old boy he believed to be our son. Her name was Lisa, and she was doing great. Afraid to ask her last name, I later wondered if I might have passed on my only chance to meet one of Ryan's organ recipients.

This chance meeting inspired me, and the following spring I decided to share our experience with others. I'm not a writer, so it was a challenge to write our story and send it to the newspapers for National Organ Donor Week. I faxed my article to three papers, and to my astonishment, all three wanted to feature it! A flurry of interviews and photo sessions followed, and we experienced an excitement we thought we were no longer capable of.

When the first article appeared, Dale and I were totally overwhelmed when we opened the paper to find that Ryan's story of hope was the banner story – right on the front page! Included in the article was the poem Ryan had written when he was seven, just as we had it inscribed on his tombstone. We wept tears of joy and sadness as we read it over and over. In his brief ten years on this earth, our son Ryan had made a difference.

A few days later, the article appeared in the other two papers, and for a few weeks we received calls from people all across Canada. Surprised but delighted, we hoped the story would help raise awareness about organ donation and perhaps inspire others to donate.

Apparently Lisa also read the article. When she saw Ryan's poem, she recognized it from a letter we sent her and realized he was her organ donor. The article said we would be at the Gift of Life medal presentation in Toronto two weeks later, so she decided to attend. Once there, she was unsure about introducing herself. We all wore name tags, and when Lisa found herself standing next to my husband Dale she couldn't hold back. You can imagine the emotional scene of hugs and tears that followed! It was truly a miraculous, unforgettable moment! It felt so wonderful to see her standing there alive and healthy, knowing that our son had helped make that possible. Ryan's kidney and pancreas had apparently been a perfect match. A part of him now lives on in her.

Moments later, a woman approached us with her eight-year-old daughter. "I think my daughter has your son's kidney," she said. Kasia was just four when both her kidneys had shut down and she had gone on dialysis. The details of her transplant matched, and we all felt certain it must have been Ryan's kidney that had given this lovely girl a new life. A few weeks later when we visited Ryan's grave, we wept tears of joy when we found a beautiful drawing left there, signed "Kasia."

Due to Canadian confidentiality laws, meetings such as these are very rare, and it is impossible to describe the intense emotions that result. When Ryan died I thought I would never feel joy again. But meeting Lisa and Kasia was a kind of miracle, opening my heart to those feelings I thought had been forever buried with my son.

Today, I now know I will always be the mother of two children. Ryan is, and always will be, part of our lives. Although, the pain of losing him will never completely leave me, I have begun putting the pieces of my life back together, though it now takes a different shape. Part of our healing came from our experience of donating Ryan's organs. I am so grateful that God allowed me to meet Lisa and Kasia so my heart and soul could reopen. Meeting them allowed me to experience that "once in a lifetime" kind of feeling again, the one I thought was gone forever.

~ *Nancy Lee Doige*

If I Can Stop One Heart From Breaking

If I can stop one heart from breaking
I shall not live in vain;
If I can ease one life the aching
Or cool one pain,
Or help one fainting robin
Unto his nest again,
I shall not live in vain.

~ Emily Dickinson

To Say Goodbye

True prayer is not asking God for love; it is learning to love,
and to include all mankind in one's affection.
– Mary Baker Eddy

It's Wednesday morning and I'm preparing to go to work. Each Wednesday for the last two years I've been visiting a patient to whom I administer comfort and massage as a practicing therapist. And each Wednesday, I wondered if it was worth it.

Several years ago, this client was referred to me by a colleague who was no longer available to treat the elderly woman. I agreed to go.

On my first visit, I found a semi-bedridden woman lying crumpled on her bed, staring lifelessly at the ceiling. My heart sank to see another human being so desolate. I introduced myself and explained to her what my treatment involved. After receiving no response, I decided the best thing to do was to go ahead without the usual formalities.

This seemingly helpless woman attempted to plant her fist right on my nose. But of course being much stronger I easily stopped her from doing any damage. At this time, the thought crossed my mind to pick up my things and get as far away from there as possible, but I had made a commitment and felt it was more prudent to honor it.

As I continued the massage, I spoke kindly and softly to the old woman. Soon she began to relax and became quiet. I then knew that my work with her could have some positive results.

And so, two and a half years later, I am leaving to go to the old crumpled lady. Mary, as she is called, doesn't try to hit me anymore and does on rare occasion smile, but is no longer able to speak. She has made little or no physical progress and by this time I'm asking myself what is the point of continuing my treatments. Each time I question my purpose in her life, I hear a small voice within my heart, urging me to continue.

On a Wednesday morning as I showered in preparation for my visit I heard a small weak voice within my inner ear. It was Mary. As clear as if she was standing right beside me I heard her say, "I'm ready to leave now."

"Hold on," I replied, "I'll be with you very soon."

When I arrived in Mary's room I found her all alone slumped over in her chair. I took her hand in mine. I saw immediately that her eyes were not in this world anymore. I put my arms around her and spoke softly in her ear. I said, "Mary, I'm here to help you. It's okay for you to leave your tired body." And then I began to sing the sacred word 'HU'. I knew that this word would help to create an atmosphere of spirituality that would make Mary's transition easier. In a moment, she took several exaggerated breaths and seconds later, she slipped away.

I knew then that I was holding only an empty shell. Mary was free.

Two and a half years, all spent to prepare for these few precious final moments. Two and a half years to share in the passing of a lovely soul. I am honored that I was chosen and I salute the life of the little, old crumpled woman.

~ *Barbara Allport*

Mothers and Daughters

A mother is the truest friend we have,

when trials, heavy and sudden,

fall upon us; when adversity takes the

place of prosperity; when friends

who rejoice with us in our sunshine,

desert us; when troubles thicken

around us, still will she cling to us,

and endeavor by her kind precepts

and counsels to dissipate the clouds of darkness,

and cause peace to return to our hearts.

– Washington Irving

An Everlasting Farewell

My mother, Alicia Jane Phinn was born on the eleventh day of the first month of the new twentieth century. Daughter of an Irish mother and a United Empire Loyalist father, she carried in her bones the determination to face her own conflicts, find her own truth, and live her own life. Inured to hardships in the pioneer life of Ontario winters and immigrant loneliness, Alicia found her own voice singing for soldiers during the First World War and for the veterans who languished in military hospitals when the fighting was over. The raw horror of that war burned in her eyes and voice when she sang, "There's a silver lining through the dark clouds shining." Her own brother had been a pilot in that war, when planes were new and "splashed on the ground like buttermilk."

Every Sunday night when my father was with his congregation at the church, my two brothers and I sat with our mother around our piano singing war songs, holding back the tears.

At eighteen, Alicia decided to become a nurse. Knowing her parents would reject her stepping out of her home, she bought a trunk and prepared her uniforms, caps and cape for her profession. Her parents got wind of her plan, forbade her leaving home, and gave her a job in a new thriving family business.

Early twenties was the era of the Flappers. With her own money, she bought stylish clothes, a Packard car, dared to be the first to bob her hair, became the soloist in her church, all within the restrictions of her family home.

When my father Andrew, a handsome young minister, arrived in Askin Street Church to preach his ordination sermon, soloist and minister looked into each other's eyes, and knew they had found their destiny. Not an easy destiny for either.

Mother, a young woman with classy shoes, classy hats, classy dresses and bobbed hair, drove into a small town in her own Packard car and found herself hated by all the mothers who hoped Andrew would choose his bride from among their daughters.

When we (my new presence did nothing to ease her outcast state) moved to another town, her first task was to persuade my father to help her return the mattresses, couches and stuffed chairs to the barn where they had come from that afternoon when the Ladies Aid was preparing the furnished parsonage for the new minister. Mother faced them when they arrived that evening to see if everything was fine.

"No," she said. "I am not used to sleeping with mice, nor with a ragged Union Jack for a tablecloth." A new bed arrived the next morning, but that was the repeated narrative of my mother's history with Ladies Aides. She fought to live her own style and her own values.

Often as we washed dishes together, she would suddenly stop, put down the sponge, fasten her hands on the sink, and gaze out somewhere beyond the window and say, "Marion, what do you think is out there beyond the clouds?" I would be struck by her beauty, pale skin, blue eyes, Irish curly hair. I felt her prison. I cried her tears alone.

The depression in the thirties bound our family into deeper dependence on each other. I now had two younger brothers and my mother had developed glandular tuberculosis from tubercular cows. For many months the congregation was unable to pay my father's small salary.

I don't remember deprivation so much as the fun we had

together collecting nuts – hickory, beech, walnut - for the winter; every thanksgiving picking cherries, strawberries, peaches, freezing or canning them. But it was hard work. My mother's condition became serious. A lump the size of an egg developed on her neck. The doctors told her they could cut it out, but she would loose the nerves on one side of her face. She would never smile again. We three children sat in silence and terror while our parents discussed what to do. (We all knew well enough what death was because the graveyard was close at hand. Our mother there!) Mother stood up, "Andrew," she said, "put some boiling water in that bowl." She brought a five-inch darning needle, sterilized it in the boiling water, and stuck it deep into the lump in her neck. Green oozed out with noxious odors. Intuitively, she had guided that needle around arteries, veins, nerves and hit her mark. From that moment I knew she would live.

These stories are essential to understand the healing, the mighty gift my mother gave me forty years later. Age was wearying her; her life-partner was gone. Stronger glasses were needed and a hearing aid. Frequently, she would phone, "Marion, that poem your father used to quote, something about 'Farewell Brutus,' can you quote it for me?" And she would write down poem after poem that she loved.

When I returned from my studies in Zurich in the summer of 1975, I realized how unwell she was. Together we went to several homes for the aged, where we saw only too clearly what lay ahead. Her proud spirit rebelled when a help-ful aide pinned a pink bow in her hair and called her "Dearie." She said nothing, but I felt her ultimate 'No'.

When we returned to the car she said, "You will never put me in a home. Promise me that."

"I promise," I said.

When Ross, Mother and I were on our way to the airport the following October as I was returning to Zurich, I knew in a flash that we would never go to the airport again together.

"I won't go, Mother," I said. "You need me here."

"Marion, if you can be free, go."

And forty-five years of our history together passed before my eyes. The freedom she fought for, the consciousness she so desperately sought, she was giving to me.

One month later, Ross phoned me in Zurich. "I'm in the hospital with your Mother. Here she is."

"Mother I'll be on the next plane. We will have tea together to-morrow night."

"Wouldn't that be lovely," she said. I knew instantly that tea was out of the question.

On the plane I dozed. I felt myself going up a canyon, following my glowing Mother who was going ahead with a lamp lighting my difficult way. I followed for some time, then had to concentrate on the sharp rocks. When I looked up for the light, it was gone. My body convulsed, scattering everything on my tray. Unconsciously I knew my Mother was dead. Consciously I did not accept it.

On arrival at the airport, I asked Ross to drive instantly to the hospital.

"She's gone," he said. I knew it, but it took months to know it.

Later in my despair, I said to him, "She could have waited. People can stay until their loved ones reach them to say good-bye. Why did she choose to go before I arrived?"

"Your mother chose her death," he said. "She said to me, 'I lived for my father, for my husband, for my children. This death is mine. If I'm here when Marion arrives, she'll care for me. I'll be a vegetable. She won't return to Zurich. This will take about two hours." Those were her last words. She began her journey into light. At the moment she died, my body convulsed on the plane.

The immensity of her gift to me – BE FREE – is etched into my soul.

When Ross and I went to her apartment, we found the poems I had quoted pinned inside her petticoat, so they would be immediately available to her.

Among them, *"Therefore our everlasting farewell take: For ever, and for ever, farewell, Cassius! If we do meet again, why, we shall smile; If not, why then, this parting was well made.*

~ *Marion Woodman*

My Mother – A Mystery

The best and most beautiful things in the
world cannot be seen or even touched.
They must be felt with the heart.
– Helen Keller

"Can I keep the minnow, Mom?" I pleaded, as the tiny creature swam frantically around the confines of my Dixie cup. "I'll take very good care of it."

"If you mean what you say, Sheila, then you'll wade into the river and set it free." It would take me years to understand what my mother meant that day. As a child, I felt I could own my prizes, even my mother, who was my best treasure. But I was wrong.

That summer, she created magic and adventure every day when she took us to the beach, down to the noisy St. Lawrence River. Following a flurry of tasks, orchestrated by my thirty-six-year-old mother, we left the farmhouse my father had rented for the summer.

Our small caravan donned white caps and stood on the grass waiting for her to take the lead. She carried Frank. Behind her Kay, carting soft drinks and diapers, took Michael's hand. Maureen toted pails, shovels, Dixie cups and a can opener, lastly I clutched sandwiches and the red Scotch blanket.

Once across the road, we marched in single file along the shoulder. Often my mother's head turned towards us to assure herself that we were following closely behind. We took a right turn one thousand feet along the highway, down a path blasted into existence and obscured by foliage. Negotiating in the loose shade of the deep descent, we grabbed tree branches to keep from falling. Before we could count to fifty, the path ended, and a panorama of wind, sand, rock and water lay at our feet.

We walked on cool, rippled sand between massive rocks until my mother found a place somewhat protected from the wind. She spread the blanket on the sand, anchoring the corners with stones. Then we ran to the river's edge to find water trapped between rocks deep enough to chill the soft drinks and scour the shoreline for seaweed to pop between our fingers. My mother stayed anchored like a stone to the blanket. She bounced Frank on her knees and collected coarse sand for Michael. We sisters leapt from one rock to another, daring each other with more difficult jumps. Our pigtails flew behind us. My mother worked frantically to create a castle that would keep my little brother Michael from the lure of the rocks. She sat there with her sons, each battling for an arm. At lunch we all ran back to the safety of the blanket. There we chose numbers to win the half bottle of red cream soda, with the losers reduced to drinking their soda from Dixie cups.

My mother never ate lunch with us, but drawing in her knees and cupping her chin, she'd listen to our adventures. When we finished eating, she'd tell Kay to sit at one end of the blanket, me at the other, placing the little ones between us. "Watch over each other; I won't be long." Off came the pink and white-striped halter and the sun skirt, and with them the trappings of motherhood.

In their stead stood a tall, handsome, big-boned woman in a black bathing suit. Without looking back at us, without pausing to test the frigid water, she'd wade in past her waist, sprinkle both shoulders with icy water and in seconds dive, disappearing into the St. Lawrence. We held onto one another on the blanket, afraid we had lost her, afraid she had left us, afraid the river had claimed her. In those long seconds I felt lonely, and small.

Then, with the grace of a dolphin she'd rise from the river with water tumbling from her dark curls and begin her swim. The smooth cutting stroke and confident rhythm of her long arms propelled this amazon into a thing of beauty that years before had captured my father's heart and now took ours. In these rarefied moments she was someone quite apart from us, and we burst with tenderness that this remarkable wet creature belonged to us. Then, perhaps for the joyous freedom she found in the river, my mother would laugh aloud, becoming once more the 'laughing Margaret' of her university days. From afar, leaning forward on the blanket, we'd sit in awe.

Yet, she always came back to us. In she'd walk, luminous, aglitter with diamond drops falling from her shoulders.

"The water was grand today," she'd say.

And that was the end of her freedom. As she sat on the blanket, the sun and wind conspired to erase the watery signs of her brief escape. What I couldn't see then was that my mother had returned to her source, just like the minnow, for the short time she left us. Once she was dressed, from the pocket of her pink skirt, she'd take three water-color paint brushes and give them to her girls; then she reached for her sandwich. We'd run to fill the Dixie cups with water, select a rock, and begin to paint water sketches that too soon evaporated. Shortly, my mother, with Frank in her arms, would lead us back up the hill.

Today, standing alone on a sandstone cliff above the St. Lawrence, whipped by steady blasts of wind rising from the mighty flow of the river, I search for my mother across the whitecaps. There was a reason for the fear I harbored of losing her when I was five. What I'd dreaded most had simply crouched, waiting behind the years, waiting for time to claim her. Yet as I turn slowly from the river and begin to climb back down the hill, I hear my mother's laughter in the gusting winds.

~Sheila Kindellan-Sheehan

Acts Of Kindness

Small acts of kindness allow me to touch souls with another person – to reach out over the great divide and brush for a moment the hand and heart of another.

An act of kindness is never wasted. It benefits the giver as much or more than the receiver. Anyone who gives with the heart strengthens the muscle within themselves; it is the aerobic training of the spirit.

I will not expect soul to just enter my life by chance. I will prepare myself, clean the vehicle that is me, resolve conflicts that tie my mind up and drain my energy. When I am less self-centered, I am able to take the personhood of another into consideration.

I enjoy being kind for kindness' sake. "And this more human love (which will consummate itself infinitely, thoughtfully and gently, and well and clearly in binding and loosing) will be something like that which we are preparing with struggle and toil, the love which consists in the mutual guarding, bordering and saluting of two solitudes."

~ *Rainer Maria Rilke*

It's A Piece of Cake

Keep your face to the sunshine
and you cannot see the shadow.
– Helen Keller

With a huge sigh of relief, I learned she would be okay. Through a series of small miracles, the endometrial cancer had been discovered early, and dealt with quickly. Her recovery was slow, but complete, and I was so grateful to God for returning her to us. I was absolutely terrified of losing my mother. We always expected her to live to be a very old lady, but she was only sixty-nine.

Then, one night after my contemplation, an inner voice said to me, clearly, and briefly: "You have five years left with your mother."

Completely astounded, I told no one. I hoped I was wrong – maybe it was fear coming from my subconscious. This was not my normal communication with spirit.

Still, I changed my relationship with her. With those words never far away, I began to cherish every moment we had. I encouraged her to take more vitamins and supplements. I changed our family dynamic and began to wrap my arms around her every time I saw her. When she called and began to rattle on, even if I were busy I would swallow my impatience, and chat – grateful that it was her voice, knowing one day it would not be there.

When the five years came and went, I decided I must

have been wrong. A year later, I had put it out of my mind altogether. Then in January 1998, exactly six years later, she was diagnosed with Acute Leukemia. She was incredibly ill, and in that moment, I knew. For some reason we'd had a reprieve, but the time was up. Totally devastated, I fell apart again. My terror of losing her was more than I could bear. I felt like a five-year-old child as I sobbed, out of control.

When her treatments began at Toronto's Princess Margaret Hospital, I began to tell her I loved her each time I left her. Uncomfortable with this simple expression of emotion, she could only pat my hand and say, "Me too."

One day I sat at home and did a focused, visualization exercise. While I sang HU, an ancient and powerful love song to God, I invited all the spiritual masters I knew to surround her hospital bed. I visualized the light from their beings filling the room, and surrounding her. Then, I turned the results over to spirit, and simply sent her all the love I had in my heart. Because of my precognition of this event, I felt it must be all part of some divine plan, and I was reluctant to interfere with it. Although it was difficult, I did not to ask them to heal her, or try and heal her myself. Somehow I managed to surrender it all to spirit.

By June it appeared the full remission we sought had been achieved. My sister arrived from B.C. with her two boys, and we had a time of love and joy as a family. We had barbeques, took a lot of pictures, and went out to dinner and the theatre. We told a lot of jokes, laughed a lot, and had a lot of hugs.

Then, in July we learned that remission had not been achieved after all. When I realized she had only three or four months left, I was overcome with grief. When she left I wanted no regrets, nothing outstanding or left unsaid, so I decided to give her my all. But giving to my mother was difficult. Her lack of self-love meant she had a hard time accepting love; low self-worth had been her lifetime companion. I sat by her bed a lot, and silently sang the HU. I became committed to helping her learn to accept my love. Perhaps it would allow her to take a bigger step when she finally did leave her body.

My sister returned in late summer, and the next day our mother, who had been home for a short while re-entered hospital. Together, we began to look for ways of giving to her what she could accept. We helped her brush her teeth, and use the bathroom. We brought her special books, and as she became weaker, we read to her. Often, we sang to her. When Ruth had to return home to her family, I carried on, doing many of the things she had done for me when I was a child. Often she said, "You need to leave now, you've done enough, I don't want you to bother with that," and the like. But every day before I left, I would put my arms around her and say, "I love you."

She began to get used to this, responding at first hesitantly and then more easily. She began to receive it, and accept it. One day she finally said, "Yes, I love you too."

Her eyes became sparkly, and when she smiled, she looked like she was lit from within. I was grateful she was not in pain, and did not require the numbing effects of narcotics. With her appetite gone, eating was a challenge, so every night I would arrive to help her eat dinner. The hospital food was abysmal, and it broke my heart to see her disappointment when confronted with it. Each day she ate less, but would not allow me to bring her anything.

Canadian Thanksgiving arrived. For many years it had been just Mum and Dad and me. I was determined we would share it one more time. Between hospital visits, I made a turkey dinner in stages. On Sunday I packed a bag with good china and silver, linen, and plastic wineglasses. I carved the bird, slicing her favorite dark meat, really thin. Then along with two TV tables, I packed and trundled it all down to the hospital on a luggage cart.

Dad was already there, and I said: "Okay you guys, I need your help. Just let me do this okay? I need you to just sit there, not fuss, and ALLOW me to do this. Okay?" Laughingly, they agreed.

I heated the food in the kitchen next door, and served the meal, giving Mum the finely sliced turkey and homemade mashed potatoes and gravy made with love. I asked my father to say the Grace, as he has always done. And then he and I watched as Mum ate every bit of food on that plate. All the work had been worthwhile, and with a lump in my throat I experienced a bittersweet kind of happiness.

Mid-week I called my sister and told her it was time. She arrived on Friday. On Sunday I accompanied my father to church, at his request. Ruth went early to the hospital, and arrived in time to be with Mum when she died that morning. Each of us was exactly where we were supposed to be.

We all have our own relationship with Divine Spirit. For some it's very overt, with a lot of inner sight, light and sound, and intimate contact with inner masters and spiritual guides. Others of us have a relationship based more on knowing, and a feeling. We are aware of how our outer life reflects the inner truths. Most of the time, I fall into this latter category.

However, I have several gifted friends in the first category. One, my dear friend Alex was at the funeral, and although I looked up hopefully into the great ceiling arches, Alex was the one who saw her. Her description of Mum appearing in a radiant peachy coral color, with a joyful smile on her face brought us a great deal of peace.

The following week I called another close, dear friend in Florida. Frannie is a 'Spiritual Intuitive' and although she works with a different line of Masters than me, she is often aware of the presence of my spiritual guide when we speak. She invited me to call her at 10:15 Friday, and before we began she would invite my mother to join us. I was a little startled, but could only agree. My mum knew of Frannie, and that she did this kind of work.

The time finally arrived, and when I called, the first thing Frannie said was, "Janet, your mother is already here. She came early to visit, and just made herself right at home. She's sitting on my bed, and we have been getting to know each other." When Frannie described her as wearing a radiant peachy coral coloured dress, I had to tell myself to keep breathing.

"She has a little dog on her lap," reported Frannie. I quickly realized it was her beloved fox terrier Laddie, from her childhood. Apparently Laddie had been waiting for her for all these years, and when she left her body, was right there to greet her with love and joy! She told Frannie she didn't go anywhere without him.

"Janet," Frannie said, "all your masters are here. There are hundreds of them – lining up and out of the doors. My house is just crackling, the energy in here is incredible! They are here with your mother, and she is being held in the higher vibration of the energy field of the masters. She couldn't be in this energy field by herself."

I had learned I would have the love and presence of the masters to escort me across the borders of death when my time came, and so would everyone that I love. The connection of the heart would allow this wonderful gift. I had always hoped it was true, but I now *know* from this experience that it *is* true!

"I'll receive information from your mother in something like balls of thought energy," said Frannie, " then I'll translate, or relay it to you. Even though your mum is still weak, and recovering from her ordeal, she is very excited about your visit. She has so much to share with you."

Through Frannie, my mother then told me how much she loved me, and how wonderful it was to have no pain, and nothing restricting her from speaking the truth from her heart. She told me how much she appreciated me, and that I stayed true to myself. She wanted me to know that during the course of her illness, as she watched me, she saw a lot of parts of herself that she did not love. The whole last five months of her life was about seeing, for the first time in her life, her true self in my eyes. In the end, that's what helped her to leave, in the pure love that came from my eyes. She had received it.

She told me in the moment she went to the light, she understood it all; in that moment everything in her life flashed before her, and she saw it like a tapestry. She instantly understood everything she'd ever heard from me, or anyone else, about spirit or truth, that she was supposed to get, but didn't, when she was here in her body. She told me she now understood why I'd get so frustrated with her, because in the body, she didn't understand it and couldn't comprehend it, because she had so much fear. She told me she stayed longer than necessary in her body for her own growth, and that during the last five months in particular, she had to do a "discovering." This involved working with some memories so she could let go of them, so these memories wouldn't hold her to the earth too long after she'd left.

She told me I needed to tell people the reason for a long illness is because the mind is not allowing the memories of the past to surface and be understood. The greater the mind's resistance to facing these issues, the longer the illness will be. She said that was why I was with her, because during her illness, my energy lifted her, and I could "hold a space" and bring the energy in to help her do this work.

She told me her leaving at this point in my life would allow me to now go and be in my life's purpose – to do what I came here to do. She told me this was all part of a divine plan we made together, before this life began. She told me that if I just remembered my own self worth, the next three months would be "a piece of cake."

She told me when she arrived on the other side, Laddie was waiting for her, along with all the members of her family that had gone before her. She was not spending too much time with them, choosing instead to go to the temple in the inner world where she is, to heal and learn. Apparently when one has had a long illness before crossing over, there is a period of time required in the inner worlds for healing, and soul goes to a kind of rest home to recover.

She told me Laddie goes nowhere without her, and she's spending her time doing higher work now. When she chooses to incarnate again, she will come back knowing the Masters' truth.

Our visit continued for over an hour, and before she left, she said how much she loved me, and she thanked me again for all the love I had given her.

Frannie then said, "She's kissing you now, it's so strange I can see her here in my room, but I can also see her there with you – there really is no separation." And then she faded, and gently and quietly left, accompanied by the masters.

This experience changed my life in a way so profound I don't even have words to describe it. The truth of everything I'd ever studied and read was validated that day. I know where my mother is, who she's with, and what she's doing. My own process of grieving had mostly been completed during her illness, and I was stunned to discover that after this experience, my healing from her loss was almost total. The love and peace which entered my heart that day stayed with me, and remains with me still.

I have three images of her; one from her life – healthy and busy being a wife and mother; one from the nine months of her illness, struggling to be in her body; and one from the present – radiant in her peachy coral blouse, reunited with her beloved Laddie, recovering and full of love in the company of the masters. It is more than I could have ever hoped. When I miss her, I think of where she is, and her final words of wisdom to me: " Just remember your own self-worth, and it will be a piece of cake."

~ *Janet Matthews*

A Life Everlasting

Mom and I were made from the same mold. The same straight brown hair, the same nearsighted brown eyes, the same physique. Mom was my mainstay. Despite all my scholastic achievements and student activities, I was shy and insecure, and she was always there for me. Mom taught social studies at my high school, so all my friends knew her and loved her too.

I was 15 when Mom was diagnosed with lupus and hospitalized for five months. She recovered and went back to teaching, and everything seemed normal. A year later she caught a simple cold that grew into a serious case of pneumonia. Within a week, she was gone. My world abruptly shattered. The door slammed shut on so many possibilities. All the questions I had had about Mom's life and feelings, about my own blossoming womanhood, about seemingly trivial things – like the recipes for our favorite Christmas cookies and Mom's famous lemon meringue pie – now none of those questions would be answered. Mom would never be there, and I was left feeling deeply sad and alone.

My whole personality seemed to change at that point. The open and idealistic person I'd been was replaced with bitterness and sarcasm. It was as if my heart was armored with grief and guilt. I was haunted by images of my mother's unhappiness. I remembered her sitting on the edge of her bed, weeping, while the rest of the family argued. I remembered so many times when it seemed I could have done more to comfort her.

In my sophomore year of college I learned to meditate and slowly began to emerge from the numbing shell of protection that I had built around myself. Meditation opened the door to dealing with my grief effectively. I'd sit with my eyes closed, and healing tears would flow.

One morning while I was meditating, I remembered caring for Mom when she had returned from the hospital. I had resented the fact that I had to dress her bedsores when I really wanted to hang out with my friends. A flood of guilt and shame welled up in me as I recalled how selfish I'd been.

Just then a thought burst into my head. It was a story Mom had told me about my grandfather, who was stricken with throat cancer, when she was eight years old. Before he died, he said to her, "Evelyn, remember this: If anything happens to me and you really need me, call and I will be there for you."

Mom told me that when she was in college, she fell in love with a young man who broke her heart. She felt so distraught that she called out to her father inside herself. She said, "Suddenly, I felt him standing in my dorm room. I felt so loved by him that I knew everything would be all right."

It seemed worth a try, so I cried out to Mom in my mind. "I'm sorry," I sobbed, over and over again. A change came over the room as time stood still. And then I felt a cloak of peace spread over me. I heard my mother say, "All is understood. All is forgiven. There is no need for regrets." At that moment all the burden of guilt I had carried around was released and replaced with a sense of freedom like I'd never felt before.

A few years later on the eve of my wedding to a wonderful man named Tony, I found myself missing Mom more that I had in years. I longed for her to share the celebration: I needed her blessing and warmth. Once again I called out to Mom to ask for her presence to be with me on my special day.

The day of the wedding was sunny and glorious – I was soon caught up in the festivities. Afterward, my long-time friend Marilyn, approached with a tear-streaked face. She said she wasn't sad; she just needed to talk to me. We made our way to a private corner of the hall.

"Do you know anyone name Forshay?" she asked.

"Well yes," I answered. "My mother's maiden name was Forshar, but it was changed from the French 'Forshay'. Why do you ask?"

Marilyn spoke more quietly then. "During your wedding ceremony, an incredible thing happened. I saw you and Tony surrounded by a light and a presence that was filled with love for you. It was so beautiful it made me cry. And I kept getting the name Forshay was associated with it."

I was too stunned to say anything. Marilyn continued, "And there was a message that came for you with it. The presence wanted you to know that you will always be loved, to never doubt that, and that this love will always come to you through you friends."

By this time, I was crying as Marilyn and I held each other. I finally understood that death could not break a connection forged in love and that my mother had always been there in spirit all these years. To this day, I will sometimes catch a glimpse of something in the eyes of friend or loved one, or even my own eyes in the mirror, and I know my mother is still here, loving me.

~ *Suzanne Lawlor*

Do It Anyway

People are often unreasonable, illogical, and self-
centered.
Forgive them anyway!
If you are kind, people may accuse you of selfish,
ulterior motives.
Be kind anyway!
If you are successful, you will win some false friends and
some true enemies.
Succeed anyway!
If you are honest and frank, people may cheat you.
Be honest and frank anyway!
What you spend years building, someone could destroy
overnight.
Build anyway!
If you find serenity and happiness, they may
be jealous.
Be happy anyway!
The good you do today, people will often forget tomor-
row.
Do good anyway!
Give the world the best you have and it may never be
enough.
Give it the best you have anyway!
You see, in the final analysis, it is between you and God.
It was never between you and them anyway!

~ *Mother Theresa*

A Glimpse of My Mother's Soul

My father passed away in the Winter of 2003. My 21-year-old daughter and I were with him at OSU (Ohio State University) medical center (my alma mater) when he passed away and it was a peaceful, grace-filled experience that we will never forget, for many reasons.

Earlier in the week, before my father died, I placed my mother in an eldercare center because she could not be left alone. She has Alzheimer's / dementia and my father had been her primary caregiver. My father needed my immediate attention in the hospital and I saw no other option.

Before we took her to the center, she required a physical exam. As my daughters and I sat in the examination room with her, listening to the doctor ask her routine questions to determine mental competency, she could answer very few. However, when he asked her to write a simple sentence the result was one that will stay with me and my three daughters forever.

When she finished writing, the doctor looked at the paper and said, "That's a wonderful sentence, Rose," and handed the paper to me. It read, 'LOVE CONQUERS ALL.'

I knew instantly that my mother had given me a gift, perhaps the greatest gift that she had ever given me – a glimpse of her soul – and a message, a profound affirmation that LOVE really is the greatest gift we can ever give each other.

I immediately left the room and sat outside in the parking lot to collect my emotions. Though it was the most difficult day of my life, putting my mother in a nursing home, I somehow knew that she understood.

~ *Carol Matthews O'Connor*

Tabitha's Song of Love

Our lives are songs; God writes the words
And we set them to music and pleasure;
And the songs grow glad, or sweet or sad,
As we choose to fashion the measure.
— Ella Wheeler Wilcox

"Mommy, all I ever want in life is to be able to sing!" It seemed like an impossible dream for our six year-old who had been born with whooping cough and a variety of related health problems. She could not do any physical activity and because we often used music to soothe her, she learned early on to appreciate the beauty and power of music.

We purchased Tabitha a kareoke machine and a microphone and never stopped encouraging her to sing even though it would cause her to go into coughing fits. I remember listening at her bedroom door at night and crying as I heard her try to sing herself to sleep in between coughing spells and seizures.

Tabitha was born six weeks premature. When the doctors whisked her away without me even touching her I knew something was extremely wrong. I learned that her lungs hadn't developed enough and she was born with "chronic cough condition." This meant that she was born with a whooping cough. The first time I was able to touch my firstborn child was many hours later that day. And even then, I could only pass my hands through the holes in the incubator while wearing sterile gloves. My heart ached for her and I wondered – how is my little girl going to grow up? It was two months later that we finally brought her home. Just two days later we had to call an ambulance. Tabitha was choking and had stopped breathing. While I watched the paramedics work over her I wondered, "What is to become of my little girl?"

We spent the better part of the next six years in and out of hospitals and doctor's offices. Because of Tabitha's weakened immune system she was susceptible to every virus going and was hospitalized constantly. She was three years old before she was able to keep solid food in her stomach – the force of the constant cough would just bring it back up again. She could not run, skip, jump, play any sports as normal children do – this was no quality of life for a child! At times the kindergarten teacher would call me to pick up Tabitha because her cough was so loud and disturbing to the class-room–I can't imagine what that was doing to her self-esteem!

By the time she was five years old, she had loss of hearing in her left ear, had developed Tourette's Syndrome and ADD (Attention Deficit Disorder). She had gone through several operations and medical specialists, and was now taking a counter-full of medications.

During that time, she'd been having a very bad spell. After consulting with the lung specialist, he told me to double the dosage of her newest medication. That was the final blow. She barely responded to her name at that point because of all the medication she was on. All I could do was hold her, rock her and listen to the music we used to play to soothe her body and mind into a restful state. She was crying, as usual, and as I looked into her bold blue eyes, I thought to myself, 'The world seems determined to destroy you. I promise you, Tabitha, I will not let you grow up like this. You are God's melody of life, and He WILL sing his song through you!'

I started my "Health Crusade."

We gradually weaned Tabitha off all medication and

started using alternative therapies. For the next two weeks she suffered through a frightening detoxification period. My heart broke as I helplessly watched as my daughter cried at me to make the pain stop. One day in particular was worse. We had already made three trips that day to our chiropractor. By dinner time, Tabitha's body was ravaged with boils and sores; her skin was raw between her toes and fingers; she was bleeding from her ears and even under her fingernails and she was shaking and kicking uncontrollably in pain! Her three year old sister Lanna, cried and begged: "Mommy, please make it stop, please help Tabitha!" My husband and I prayed for a miracle.

Our chiropractor rushed to our house that evening and massaged her, not leaving her side until after three a.m. when Tabitha finally collapsed into sleep. The chiropractor told us later that she had never witnessed a child go through so much pain. But from that point on, she started to improve.

I read every book, attended every seminar, and talked to as many alternative health professionals as I could. For seven years, we experimented with alternative therapies such as chiropractic, massage, psychological counseling, nutritional supplements, the food she would eat, the stress in her life. We even had to purify the air in her for two hours a day and keep her confined during that time. We had charts all over the house – it was like trying to find a secret recipe; a little bit of this, a little less of that. My heart was in my mouth every time we tried something new.

At twelve years old, Tabitha's cough had improved to a nervous tick – that meant that she would shake and have a small cough similar to clearing your throat but it was constant. Then a friend of mine, introduced me to a program by a leading expert in human cell technology – Dr. Myron Wentz. I agreed to research it and when looking over the material I heard a pounding at the door of my heart telling me this could be the answer to our prayers.

We started Tabitha on the program immediately, and

within a few short weeks, she had improved to where there was no cough, no nervous tick, no Tourette's symptoms, and no ADD symptoms. Nothing!

Today, Tabitha's dreams are all coming true. She was invited to sing at an International Convention, in front of 5,000 people. Tabitha received three standing ovations as I watched from the side, tears rolling down my cheeks.

Since then, Tabitha was recorded on a CD. She sings regularly in our church choir and at weddings. She sang in eight performances of a Christmas play that was featured on our local cable TV, for the mayor and youth of our community, and has received many awards for vocal competitions. To top it off Tabitha now teaches vocal and piano lessons to younger children.

She is our voice from heaven and a testament to the fact that dreams do come true if you never give up hope!

~ *Nancy Lacasse*

.

Healing the Past

If I Could

Nothing beats love. Love is the greatest healing power there
is, nothing else comes close. Not ancient cures, modern
medicines and technologies, or all the interesting books we
read or the wise things we say and think.
Love has a transformational power.
– Naomi Judd

I was born at home in the charming little fishing village of
Lower Largo, Fife, in Scotland. Like Robinson Crusoe, the
hero of Daniel Defoe's famous children's story, I have always
had an adventurous spirit. Interestingly enough, the story of
Robinson Crusoe is based on a true episode in the life of a
sailor named Alexander Selkirk, who was born in Lower Largo
in 1676. A statue erected in his memory still stands today, and
the Crusoe Hotel is within walking distance of our old home.

Because my dad was in the hospital recovering from a
hernia operation, my Grandmother, an aunt, and a midwife
attended my birth. Like most European men at that time, my
dad wanted his first-born to be a son. When he learned he
had a daughter, he was extremely disappointed. So, when my
brother came along a year later, he became the apple of my
father's eye. He was my dad's favorite and could do no wrong,
while I was often made to feel stupid and worthless.

Dad was a very strict Presbyterian minister who strongly
believed in corporal punishment. Throughout my childhood,
I was frequently subjected to severe thrashings for my

brother's misdeeds as well as my own. Eventually I become so angry and resentful, I began to wish my father would die.

Later we moved to the beautiful Highlands of Scotland where the mountains are as high as the Lochs are deep. It was in this lovely setting that my dad wrote the history of our clan, the MacMillans, and composed some incredibly beautiful music. There were times when he could be very kind, but the bitterness I had toward him blinded me to his good qualities. When I was nineteen, I fell in love with a young man of a different religion, and dad threatened to disown me if I married him. Heartbroken, I complied with his wishes, and broke it off.

For a time I considered moving to Australia, but eventually moved to Canada, where I met and married my present husband. We settled in Kitchener-Waterloo, in the province of Ontario. I came to realize that all the anger I held for my Dad was like a poison to my system, and that by holding onto it, I was harming only myself. I was tired of feeling bitter, angry and resentful, but although I really wanted to forgive him I didn't know how.

In desperation, I asked God for help. Soon afterward a woman came into my life just long enough to teach me how to do a spiritual exercise for love and forgiveness. I learned that spiritual exercises help us to build up our spiritual strength, so we can let go of the past, and grow spiritually. Each day as I went into contemplation, I visualized myself walking towards my dad and saying, "I love you and forgive you for all the pain you have caused me in the past." And then I would give him a big hug. As time went on, my heart began to heal and the hardened concrete-like barrier began to let go. For the first time in my life, love and forgiveness flooded in.

Shortly after this my parents decided to visit us in Canada. I was anxious to see if my dad would notice the changes in me. As my dad stepped off the bus that had brought them from the airport, I saw tears of love in his eyes.

With arms outstretched he hugged me with a depth I'd never experienced from him before. I was overjoyed.

One day, he brought home a new friend for dinner. As I prepared the meal I overheard Dad's friend say, "You have a beautiful daughter, Mr. MacMillan." My heart leapt with joy when Dad replied, "It's not her outer beauty that's important, it's her inner beauty that counts."

After my parents left, we kept very close through our correspondence. Sadly, a year and a half later, my dad passed away. I had always hoped that he might say he was sorry for the hurt he had caused me, but that never happened.

Some years later, the Clan MacMillan held their international gathering in Vicksburg, Mississippi. Forty-one years ago, Dad had visited Vicksburg to promote the Clan MacMillan in the USA, and for many years served as a bard, historian and Chaplain for clan members all over the world. Because of this, the clan decided to honor his memory by having a concert featuring some of his music. They also decided to make Dad's favorite MacMillan tartan, the official tartan throughout the eleven-day gathering.

I flew down to Vicksburg to be guest of honor for this important event, and was asked to give a series of speeches on growing up with my dad. Faced with this challenge, I decided to totally rewrite my life from the high viewpoint of love, leaving out all the childhood abuse. I focused on all the lovely moments I had spent with my dad. By the time I had finished writing, I felt as though I had died as the person I was, and had been reborn anew. It was as if all the pain and bitterness was washed completely away.

Throughout the whole gathering I felt the presence of my dad's love constantly. Through the wonderful stories the old people shared with me about my dad, and through listening as Dad's music was performed by various musicians, I came to have a new appreciation for him.

On the last night of the gathering, we stayed at a Bed and Breakfast in Jackson. I awoke at 4:15 a.m. with a strange feeling of expectation that something wonderful was about to happen. The clock radio came on suddenly, as a man's melodious voice filled the room. Like a warm sweet caress the words sang out, 'If I could turn back the hands of time, I'd hold you close because you're mine, and I'd tell you how precious you are... I love you!'

Tears of joy flowed freely. The residue of pain in my heart was now completely healed, and in its place an incredible feeling of divine love and gratitude.

Love holds no boundaries. It crosses all borders and repairs even the most damaged heart.

Dad, I love you too.

~*Sybil Barbour*

Healing Blade

I stood, spade in hand, preparing to dig in the moist soil. My plan was to widen the edge of the garden to make space for still more perennials and annuals. I stood on the shovel, putting my weight behind the long blade, and pushed into the soil. Pulling back the sod, I noticed an object exposed in the dirt. Picking it up, I studied the form enclosed in a clay-like cocoon.

Gardening had been a favorite pastime of my parents, long ago, when we all lived together as a family in our Scarborough, Ontario home. This is where Mom and Dad found a common ground in an otherwise tumultuous daily life. In June, we took the traditional trip to the nursery where Mom and Dad would purchase the seasons supply of annuals and perennials, peat moss and loam, while my two brothers, sister and I played in the small amusement area.

Gardening was a form of communion for my parents, a sacred ceremony of placing new plants in the prepared soil where all could witness the cycle of growth and beauty that only nature can produce. Those were moments when the unpleasant turmoil of our home-life was out of mind and I could feel some safety, stability and a sense of richness.

Money seemed to always be a source of unspoken stress in our home. Although it was rarely discussed openly, it was clear to me that we were not affluent. We had a home and nice clothes and even took a summer holiday, but behind all this was a feeling of lack and especially that my father wanted more.

Those two aspects of my home life followed me as I grew up, both the financial strain and the love of gardening. That constant source of stress I'd experienced over money in our family, became a kind of sad legacy for me when I moved out. I could never seem to make ends meet no matter how hard I tried. I watched as my friends and acquaintances flourished in their homes while I lived on the poverty line.

It was springtime, thirty years later. I stood on the front lawn of my mother's home. She and Dad had long since divorced – and he, married for the third time, now lived several blocks away. Divorced myself, I'd returned home for a time, to heal and recover from a long and difficult period of my life.

Recognizing the presence of some treasure, I began to pick and prod at the hard clay form in my hand, very soon exposing the outline of what looked like a penknife. I took the knife inside where I soaked it in salt and water for several days, until the white mother of pearl hull was fully exposed.

I was certain the insides were rusted shut, but took it upon myself to try to open it. Three days later, after randomly filing and digging between the blade and the edge, I was able to pull out the blades. To my amazement they were fully intact, but coated in a sticky substance. Taking a steel wool pad, I scrubbed away the white tacky film that covered the blades from thirty years underground. Very soon, the stainless steel surface of the blades was shimmering and clean.

When I asked my mother about the knife, she recalled it had belonged to my father. I began to remember years before, how my father would pack this very knife when he'd gone on trips with the Fin and Feather Hunting and Fishing Club. Later my brothers used it for games, to throw at wooden beams, and to play cowboys and Indians. I never noticed its absence when it had just gone missing.

I felt compelled to return the knife to my father and got in my car for the five-minute drive. Dad, now retired, answered the door in his typically casual manner. I handed him the knife ceremoniously, half expecting some sort of crescendo after all my efforts. His reply was anticlimactic. "That knife belonged to my Father," he said with what seemed little emotion. He told me a little about the history of the knife and we parted. I felt disappointed. Certainly after all my efforts, there must be more.

A few days later I called him for something. I began questioning him about his father, prodding him like I'd prodded the old knife. I learned a great deal about what had shaped my father's attitudes that afternoon and what had fed the feeling of poverty I carried for my forty years.

At the age of ten, Dad's life changed in an instant when his older sister happened by chance to sit next to my grandfather and his "date" in the local movie theatre of the small Ontario town they lived in. Granddad's affair ended my grandparent's marriage. Afterward, Dad's dream of becoming a pharmacist like his father faded away. Taking odd jobs, my grandmother struggled to make ends meet, but with no support from her now ex-husband, college for Dad was out of the question.

My grandfather wanted nothing to do with my dad or the family. I'd never met my grandfather and hadn't heard much about him until now; I'd only experienced the bitterness my father carried in his heart as a man. I'd never understood that he had once had a father too, who'd turned his back on his only son.

My dad continued to tell the story of how my grandmother had struggled to raise my dad and his three sisters with odd jobs. It was a great strain. Once she'd managed to save fifteen-hundred dollars for a down payment on a house. Fifteen-hundred dollars was an enormous amount in the 1940s. She naively handed it to a land developer who absconded with her savings, leaving my dad and his sisters to live in a tent that summer. I recalled stories Dad had told me as a child, one in particular where he'd stolen a can of beans out of dire necessity and starvation, only to find when he finally got it open that it was rotten.

Most of my life, I'd struggled with money, carrying a burden of poverty, unable to break the cycle even after many attempts. As I listened to the story of my dad's life, I began to understand so much about myself, my poverty, my inability to get ahead, and those deep beliefs buried in my subconscious.

The knife seemed to have surfaced to show me a healing was in process. I'd carried the cutting wounds of my father and his mother. His estrangement from his father had meant years of poverty and hurt, which in turn had been passed down to me.

Now it was time to let go of the wounds of my past and my father's father's past and to let love enter my heart. I said good-bye to my dad, now a little more compassionate and understanding of what had shaped his views and caused him to have such a tough exterior. Soon after, I saw my grand-mother in a dream. She'd passed on some years before. 'Grammy' had some of that bitterness in her till the end. In the dream we ran to each other and hugged warmly as my dad looked on. The familiar bitterness was gone and now only compassion and understanding remained.

The garden is a treasure that yields its beauty unselfishly. Our family was rich in a way I hadn't realized. The knife represented the past, buried anger and resentment in my family home. Through learning to forgive my father for his seeming hardness of heart, I could step forward into a new life of abundance and greater love.

~Darlene Montgomery

Once Upon a Birthday

When I was a little girl, growing up on the southern Manitoba prairies, I would sometimes hurry from our yard, dash up the path and bounce up onto the sidewalk, where I would steal a stroll along the walk, until someone appeared, then I would quietly return to the grassy curb or the gravel. Although not one person was ever unkind, the feeling came from within me – I don't belong to this place. And so when I accidentally discover I was adopted, I wasn't surprised at all.

The Canadian prairies and its people were slow to embrace change so, when I was growing up, right or wrong, illegitimacy was still an ugly thing. People of my town, and my adopted parents were wonderful to me. Keeping the secret from me about my origins was done with the very best of intentions.

As an adult I learned that I was the illegitimate child of my adopted mother's niece – no big deal. It was not an unheard of story – my biological mother had been married, had four children, then lost her husband suddenly to a car accident. Afraid and alone, she soon found herself penniless and pregnant by a man who didn't want her or her brood of children. She made an honest attempt to keep me after my birth, but soon came to realize the impossibility of her situation, so she offered me to my adopted parents to raise as their own.

So I changed everyone's life. Phyllis, my birth mother, and my half siblings were never mentioned. No family member ever committed the grievous sin of speaking her name in my presence. Not one cousin, aunt or in-law ever broke the wall of silence my parents built around me. I learned she was my mother at the age of seventeen, but it took until I was twenty-four to learn where she lived and obtain a phone number. When that day came, elated and reckless, I called her immediately.

We hit it off at once. She sounded kind and warm, and I was drawn to her voice on the telephone with a force I couldn't identify. We made plans to meet in Alberta, where she lived with her husband and where most of her six other children also lived. At the last moment, for many reasons, but chiefly because I lacked the courage to go through with it, I didn't go.

She was terribly hurt, and felt betrayed. She had confessed her past to her children, and I had let her down. I knew that I had destroyed perhaps my only opportunity to have a relationship with my blood family. We never spoke again.

Indifferent to my pain, the years flew by. I teetered between periods of putting the whole thing behind me, to zealous attempts to find my mother and my siblings, neither of which bore any fruit. After a while, it became more like a lie than the truth. From time to time I would torment my adopted parents with questions about my biological family, but they battened down the hatches and pulled the shade of secrecy, just as they had always done.

Otherwise, life was good. I was married to a great guy. With two young children we were a happy, busy family with a farm only twenty-five miles from where I grew up. Our house was filled with laugher and love and I was contented.

Then, in the fall of 1994, everything began to unravel. I became ill.

Sicker than I had ever been in my life, I had constant, terrible pain in my abdomen. I was terrified, weak and nauseated. I lost weight, my hair began to fall out, I cried constantly and I was obsessed with my health. I became convinced beyond a doubt that I had cervical cancer, and that it was advanced to a stage beyond treatment. Fear and pain dominated my existence. I couldn't take care of my family, and for the first time in my life I was too frightened to see a doctor. I seldom left our home.

My poor husband was completely at a loss. When not pleading with me to see a doctor, he cared for the children most of the time. Inevitably, I hit bottom, and in mid-December, I called my family doctor, after hours, and weeping uncontrollably, told him of my condition. A thorough physical examination proved me to be absolutely healthy, but I was suffering from a nervous breakdown.

Christmas 1994 saw me on medication and receiving treatment from a psychologist I knew personally. Together she and I searched for the cause of my mysterious emotional problems, and settled on my adoption and separation from my biological mother as the probable culprit. We talked and talked and gradually my demons began to retreat.

By July 1995, as well as being a seasoned veteran of counseling, I was also completely back to myself. The circumstances of my birth no longer haunted me, I had discovered that I loved and need my biological mother as much as I needed my adopted parents, and that was okay. I decided that now was the time to find her again, this time I knew things would be different. But when I told my adopted parents of my decision, I was stunned to hear that she had died the year previously. They were unsure of the circumstances, except that it was an illness, and I had not been told because of my emotional state at the time.

The news hung in the air for what seemed like an eternity, and slowly I began to realize that I already knew what had happened to her. She had died from cervical cancer. I contacted her sister, the person who had provided me with her phone number all those years before, and she confirmed my intuitions.

I was left alone again, with the ghostly presence of a woman I never knew, but knew intimately. Finally, I understood the source of my pain the year before. Tears fell down my face in recognition of the fact that as my mother lay dying, I had shared her pain and anguish. I had wrestled with her fears. We were together in her death, just as we had been in my birth, and I realized what a wonderful gift my birth mother had bestowed upon me.

December 2000, my biological sister found me through the Internet, after I had given up all hope of ever finding my siblings. Our reunion was amazing. I felt an immediate connection to my three brothers and three sisters. We rejoiced to have all of us together. Whatever grief there may have been left in my heart was healed. In my sister's words, "We are seven." A current that was the soul and spirit of our mother runs through us all, binding us together.

I have talked at great length with them all about our mother's life and death. I discovered through my siblings, a woman who was funny, full of mischief, loved animals, was generous and played hard at life. I learned that my mother did, indeed die of cervical cancer for which she refused treatment and pain medication. She entered the hospital only a couple of days before her death, and according to her nurse, held onto life by a weak thread and strong determination until she finally passed away on the 29th of December, 1994, my 32nd birthday! Our lives are like the Psalm Ecclesiastes 3:1: 'To every thing there is a season, and a time to every purpose under the heaven..'

Today my husband and I have a fourteen-year-old daughter, a twelve-year-old son, and a seventeen-month-old daughter who is full of mischief and life, loves animals and plays hard at everything she does.

~ *Debbie McMechan*

Becoming Conscious

Other people may be there to help us, teach us,
guide us along our path.
But the lesson to be learned is always ours.
Melody Beattie

As I stood at the phone listening to the news from my husband that my mother had just had a heart attack, I was stunned. We'd been instructed to have no outside contact during the week of the workshop, so when I received a message that my husband had called in the first hour of the program, I was extremely upset.

The whole reason I'd come to the weeklong workshop in 1979 was to finally have healing on issues surrounding the volatile relationship with my mother. Years of trying to prove myself and longing for her acceptance had kept us alternating between times of joy and frequent periods of distancing. I was third of eight children and from a very young age had heard her say repeatedly she had only ever wanted two children. I believed I had always been a burden to her.

In early 1993, I had to release her from her job in my company and she began what resulted in a four-year "drought", barely speaking to me and leaving the room if I came in. My sense of abandonment and inadequacy soared. Missing my family's gatherings and knowing she would never give in, I reluctantly took all responsibility for the problems to make peace with her. It didn't solve the underlying issues and within weeks I knew that not much had changed. On an impulse, I visited a psychotherapist I knew to ask the question, "Do people ever get over this stuff?" She pointed me towards a workshop that claimed to offer healing of childhood pain. I was ready.

I'd been there only an hour when the call came from my husband. When he said "Your mother had a heart attack this morning," I was stunned. Her life was in danger and I was terrified she would not make it. I felt so helpless.

Then I was shocked at a surge of anger rising within me. I'd finally found the courage to deal with what I perceived to be her dominance, her criticism, her rejection, her rage – all the behaviors that I believed had scarred my life and somehow she'd managed to find a way to interfere. How could she do this to me?

Sadness and fear overwhelmed me and I sobbed uncontrollably on my bed. I felt completely unable to decide what to do and the course instructors let me know that I would have to make the choice. Left alone, a peacefulness began to fill my room. I could feel my mother's presence as I sat by myself. Holding my breath, I felt her warmth and protection encompassing me. She said clearly, not so much in words but as an impression, "Come home. You don't have to do this – it'll be too painful. Come home."

I was shaken by the message and startled by how it had come to me. Then I realized that my mother was throwing me a lifeline. I was witnessing, first hand, how we can communicate on a spiritual level. My mother wanted to protect me from the pain that she knew I was about to face.

I breathed deeply and decided to continue with the workshop. I silently thanked my mother and told her that I had to do this. It was an enormous turning point as I made the choice to do what was right for me. I decided in that moment that I would now live in a conscious way instead of hiding from feelings and thoughts.

Darlene Montgomery

Tranquility came over me. In my more composed state I was able to call home for an update. As if somehow the divine hand of God had intervened in these events I learned my mother was out of danger and would be okay. The work I did that week changed my life and how I would forever see my mother. I truly understood that she had done the best she could. I no longer needed to blame her for the past or the present.

When I visited her a week later she had just been released from the hospital. As I entered the room our eyes met. Instantly our worlds came together in a profound new way. Her face was so incredibly calm and she had a quiet glow of awareness that I doubt anyone else noticed. I knew without any doubt that our relationship would never be the same. Kneeling in front of her, we held each other warmly, neither wanting the moment to end. I will never forget how it felt to have her hold me with so much tenderness. It seemed as if we were starting our lives together all over again. For the first time, we were consciously giving each other real love, honest and pure.

This reunion was important as it gave us strength for what lay ahead.

My father had been undergoing cancer treatments and within days was told that he had only a few weeks to live. Each afternoon I spent time with him at the hospital and in the evenings I stayed with my mother. I listened with sincere compassion as she poured out the stories of their life together and how terrifying the future looked. The groundwork had been laid for our bonding. I no longer heard the mother I'd resented and feared, but the voice of a woman living in pain and anguish. My experience gave me the tools to support her and I cherish the time we shared.

Life is still full of challenges and sometimes I feel myself slipping into old patterns with my mother. When I do, I close my eyes and see the beginning of my conscious journey. Once again, I am on the side of a bed those many years ago, remembering and honoring the power of a mother and daughter's love.

~ *Daryl Wood-Clarke*

New Beginnings

There is a light in this world, a healing spirit

more powerful than any darkness we may encounter.

We sometime lose sight of this force when

there is suffering, and too much pain.

Then suddenly, the spirit will emerge

through the lives of ordinary people

who hear a call and answer

in extraordinary ways.

– Mother Teresa

Another Chance at Life

Everyone has been made for some particular work,
and the desire for that work has been put in every heart.
— Rumi

I'd been a schoolteacher for many years in Washington, DC. At the time I was working as the vice-principal of an elementary school. I'd been experiencing some chest pain, and because the flu had been going around our school, I thought that's what I had. When it did not go away after several weeks, I went to the emergency ward to have it checked. The doctor said he didn't like the sound of my heart, and recommended I get a CAT scan. I made an appointment, but because his reaction was so low-key, I never gave it much thought.

It was a beautiful sunny day when I arrived at the diagnostic center for my CAT scan appointment. The technicians injected me with a kind of a dye, and then told me to breathe and hold, breathe and hold. Soon I began to feel kind of nauseous and asked, "Is this normal?"

They told me it would only be a bit longer and to hold on. Finally they said, "We're through now. We'll be back to tell you what the results are." I lay back and waited for them to return. Then suddenly my inner voice told me, 'Something isn't right.'

After what seemed a very long time, the technicians returned, and said in a serious tone, "Miss Rice, we have your doctor on the phone."

I said, "Oh my gosh. Something's not right!" Slowly I got off the table and walked over to the telephone. My doctor told me, "They're going to rush you to the hospital. You're having an aortic aneurysm. It happened while you were there in the clinic. Don't be alarmed."

I tried to calm myself down while slowly getting dressed. I called my husband, and he started out to meet me. By the time I finished dressing the ambulance had arrived.

They were taking me to Doctor's Hospital, but on the way a request came through from my cardiologist who was on call. He didn't want me at Doctor's Hospital, and re-directed the paramedics to take me to University Hospital.

They rushed me into emergency, and then down into the ICU (Intensive Care Unit). My husband had been following the ambulance, and arrived at that moment. The ICU was down in the dungeon, and had low lights and no windows. It was a very dismal place. I thought, 'Oh my gosh, what's happening to me?'

In that moment, I turned it over to God. As I did, I began to experience a sort of inner peace in the midst of all the chaos. I couldn't believe I was going through this but I wasn't scared. They hooked me up to the heart monitor and made all the usual preparations. The CAT scan at the hospital had revealed I had an "aortic dissection" which is a tear in the aorta, the main artery of the heart. It was extremely serious, so much so they could not repair it without me losing my life.

I was immediately put on heavy medication to bring my blood pressure down, and remained in the ICU. After twenty-two days I was responding to treatments and getting better. Once they got my blood pressure stabilized for a given period, they decided I was strong enough to come out of ICU. During this time they continued doing tests. It seems my blood had taken another route to get itself through my body. They were giving that a chance to heal or to do whatever it had to do.

Finally I was well enough to be moved up to the fourth floor where the rooms were much better. I was just happy to get out of the dismal dungeon. I was in my new room for two days, everything seemed well and I was thinking I would be out of there soon.

Then one evening, an attendant started talking about the hospital and how she didn't really care for it. When she commented, "I wouldn't bring a dead horse here," I said to myself, 'Oh no! Why is she saying this to me? Why is she trying to make me feel unsure about things? I'm getting better. I'm almost out of here. Everything has seemed fine so far.'

The following night, after the midnight nurse left, the next shift of nurses never arrived. I kept ringing for the nurse but she didn't come. All of sudden I began to feel very weak and was having a hard time breathing. Although I'd been walking by then, I was suddenly too weak to stand and no one was coming. I knew my blood pressure was skyrocketing.

I tried getting an outside line to call my husband. Normally, it was almost impossible to get an outside line, but that night I got one on the first try. Richard was in bed, and answered in a low, barely audible voice. " Richard, you've got to get here right away," I begged, " I'm dying. I just know I will die if you don't get here."

"I'll be right there," he said, and began moving quickly.

No one was coming to give me any medicine. No one was helping. I was weak and felt dreadful. And throughout the remainder of the night no one came.

I realized dawn was coming. And then I heard Richard's voice saying, "Why aren't you helping my wife!" The nurse who had heard me calling for help earlier in the night decided she'd bring my medication now. By that time I was about to lose it. I took it, and then I started having a high fever. The nurse now looking extremely concerned said, "Here's your blood pressure medicine, just in case your blood pressure may be up."

By this time my husband looked at her and demanded, "Who's the doctor on call?" No one seemed to know. Richard ran into the hall hysterically calling code blue and yelling, "She's dying. Get her some help right now!"

That got their attention. Everyone started running in circles. They couldn't find the emergency cart or the paddles and they didn't know which doctor was on duty. It was total chaos. My husband was still calling code blue, but still, no one was doing anything to help me.

I began passing out. At last a few doctors ran into the room and I said, "You doctors better not let me die." And then I called out, "Richard where are you?"

"I'm right here," he answered.

"Richard," I said, "I'm going. And I just want you to know that I love you. I know I'm going out and I don't know whether I'll get back, but I love you."

And then everything went black.

Immediately I was aware of being in a setting like the Grand Canyon. It looked like an Indian reservation, and there were no people around. Beside me was an old, very tall pine tree. I looked up and saw at the top a beautiful eagle gazing down at me. I looked into its piercing eyes and found myself flying towards him – and then I merged into him. I became the eagle, and was soon soaring through the canyon on eagle's wings. I felt free – freer than I had ever felt before!

As I swooped down, I saw liquor bottles and needles on the ground, I thought, "These people have destroyed themselves with drugs, alcohol and tobacco. But where are they? What happened to them?"

I never did see them. But I felt that my Indian heritage had some connection. "Am I supposed to do something to help the Indian people?" I wondered. "Is this a sign I'm supposed to help them?"

Then suddenly, I was transported to another scene. I was sitting in the middle of an enormous movie theatre. Again, I was alone, and the big white screen in front of me was blank. Then a kind of knowingness came over me. 'Oh!' I thought. 'I've got a chance to write my own script in my new life, whatever that's going to be.'

Suddenly I was back in the hospital, with people moving around me. I was in my light body – I was just light. Nobody could see me, but I could see them. I began hearing voices say, "Elizabeth ... Miss Rice." And then, "She's coming back. I think she's coming back."

I moved toward the voices. I was excited and said to myself, 'I'm back where I was!' Then everyone was very excited and saying, "She's coming back! She's coming out of it! Miss Rice. You're back! – Miss Rice, welcome back. Welcome back!"

I opened my eyes and saw those old tiles and thought, 'Oh I must be alive. I must be back in the dudgeon ... back in ICU.'

I wasn't aware of being hooked up to the respirator. I was trying to talk but couldn't. I was trying to say, "Take this off of me." I gestured for some paper and a pen. Someone brought them, and I started to write uncontrollably. I was writing letters to people. I couldn't spell and at first they had no idea what was going on.

I was in between two places, trying to express what I was feeling in knowing I had a second chance at life.

I was saying, "I love you," to my husband, and, "Thank God I'm still here."

I even tried to joke with my family members who were there by now, but the words came out garbled on paper. My sister-in-law caught on and said, "Betty's joking!"

The others said, "No! It can't be." But it was true. I was trying to express the humor of something I had experienced. I just continued to write beautiful things to everyone and to feel the most incredible gratitude for my life.

A week later I was released from hospital. After I recovered I began to wonder, 'God, what in the world am I supposed to be doing?' I began looking for answers to explain my experience. I knew there was something very important I was meant to do. In my quest to understand the Indian reservation I had seen, I discovered my grandmother, who was part Cherokee and part Irish, had started a foundation fifty years before called *Tomorrow's World Foundation*. Her name had been Elizabeth Bell-Jones.

My grandmother, my mother and I were all named Elizabeth. My grandmother had been adopted by a white family and given a very good education. She'd eventually graduated from university. Grandmother had been an inspirational woman who kept the company of some very renowned individuals. She'd invented a system of education, especially for children of poverty, based on a five-pointed star. Its basis was to teach kids self-esteem and literacy and to give them a well-rounded education to empower them.

As I looked closely at my near death experience with the Indian reservation and the devastating living conditions I had seen there, I felt somehow my grandmother's legacy was being passed down to me. I re-established *Tomorrows' World Foundation Inc.*, a non-profit organization stressing educational, social, spiritual, physical and financial empowerment with a focus on African Americans and other minorities.

I'm in the process of researching my grandmother's life and writing a book about my experience. I know my near-death experience was an opportunity to have a chance to make a real difference here on earth. I know part of that difference is to help others to rise above the conditions of poverty through education and awareness.

Time is an illusion. It will fool you. It will trap you! You need to do things in the here and the now. If you have a dream, the time to do it is now!

~ *Elizabeth Rice*

Jump of Faith

When you follow your bliss...doors will open where
you would not have thought there would be doors;
and where there wouldn't be a door for anyone else.
— Joseph Campbell

I'd been backpacking through New Zealand, having left my
law practice two months earlier. The trip was a continuation
of the journey of the self-discovery I'd been on for the last two
and a half years. I'd become a self-help junkie, as I desperately
sought what I wanted to do with my life. In the process, I'd
read dozens of books, attended scores of workshops and
lectures. It was difficult to practice family law while undergoing this intense inner searching, so I gave myself a deadline of
Christmas 1996, at which time I planned to leave law behind
and take refuge in the green and clean land of the kiwi.

In addition to being an oasis of beauty, New Zealand is a
thrill-seeker's paradise. At every stop, travelers are bombarded
with ads for a myriad of outdoor adventures: bungy jumping,
white-water rafting, caving, sand dune tobogganing. I had
decided to do a glacier hike, a wild speedboat ride, some cave
walking, maybe a helicopter tour. As for the really dangerous,
really radical stuff, no thank you. I like my feet on terra firma
... so then why is it that everywhere I went I couldn't take my
eyes off the ads for tandem skydiving?

Why was I so incredibly drawn to the ads considering it
was something that I was never going to do?

The small town of Taupo, New Zealand, on the shores of beautiful Lake Taupo, is famous for its tandem skydiving. On my travels there a force seemed to come over me. Before I realized what I was doing, I'd signed up for a jump, scheduled for the next day.

As the evening wore on, the enormity of my decision began to weigh on me. What had I done? Was I completely mad? Had I forgotten about the article in the paper three weeks earlier about the tandem pair whose parachute had failed to open? Right here in Taupo?

I could still back out … no – I had backed down on too many challenges in my life. I felt very certain of one thing. I had to do this.

That night I couldn't sleep. I was a nervous wreck. My stomach was in knots – my heart was racing. In my mind, I was falling, trying to grasp thin air. My breakthrough finally came at five in the morning. What was I afraid of? Death. Yes, it was death that scared me. Suddenly I saw my life. I had lived well. I had loved. I had laughed. I had cried. I had pushed through my fears and doubts and had left the legal world for the thrill of an unknown future.

I already was a success. Jumping out of an airplane had been the one thing I thought I would never do. Now I was doing it. If I died, I would die knowing that I had overcome the greatest fear of my life. A calm descended over my body, and I fell into a sound sleep.

The next morning we drove out to the airfield. No paved runways, just grass. In the hangar, I saw the plane. That's the plane? It had one seat for the pilot and a few feet of floor space for the jumpers. No standing room – just sitting on the floor.

I paid my money, signed a waiver, put on my coveralls, soft helmet and goggles, and tried to stay calm. Impossible. My heart was pounding. Every nerve was on end.

Ascending, I tried to think about where I was and what I was about to do. Just going on a nice airplane ride. My tandem guide Greg strapped me to his body. He was behind me. He had the parachute. In about seven minutes we were up to our prescribed altitude of 10,000 feet. The door flew open. The first pair of jumpers edged their way over to the door. In a second they were gone. Now it was our turn. Without thinking, I shuffled to the door. Don't look down. Two miles of nothing. Sitting in the doorway, I hooked my legs under the body of the plane. Greg yelled out "Big banana" and I arched my back. He yelled something else and we were gone.

We were falling. Everything was spinning. In a few moments, we stabilized. Two bodies, spread-eagled, horizontally rushing through space. Soon we hit terminal velocity, 200 kilometers an hour – 1000 feet every five seconds. It didn't feel like we were falling anymore, rather that we were suspended in midair, except the wind was roaring in my ears, the pressure on my face incredible and the ground was getting closer. Thirty seconds of free fall. Suddenly I felt a gentle tug and we were upright. The chute had opened. Thank you Greg. Thank you God.

There was a perfect silence and we floated down softly. With shaky hands, I took my camera out of my coveralls and snapped a few photos. After a smooth landing, I hugged Greg, and thanked him for his strength, his skill and his calm reassurance.

Back in town, I was walking on clouds. I had done it! I was forever changed. I had faced my greatest fear. I had jumped out of an airplane. I knew that there was nothing, nothing, I could not do. While I still couldn't see the particulars, I knew my life was about to begin.

That courage emboldened me several months later to begin my own business as a holistic career consultant and life purpose coach. I know why I was irresistibly drawn to those ads. Knowing what was in store for me, my higher self was preparing me, helping me to develop the courage I would need to leap forward with my dreams.

And now when I speak to groups, or to my clients, I share this advice. Listen to your intuition. Follow your leads. Face your fear and trust. The universe will bring you everything you need. I guarantee it!

~ *Carol Le Neveu*

Winds of Change

It is instinctive to resist change. We fear those things that change implies – endings – the unknown. Change disrupts comfort and security. It precipitates new areas of learning and adjustment, which often requires effort or hard work. Change challenges our inherent skills. It forces growth, and that can be painful.

At 4 pm on March 3, 2002, my life changed forever. Traveling at 60 mph on the highway in my convertible, loaded with 5,000 Beyond Reason Magazines, I hit a stopped transport truck. It isn't that I have been scarred or permanently crippled. Nor did I endure a great deal of pain or suffering. In fact, throughout the crash, I seemed almost shielded and protected. And I recovered almost miraculously within a very short period of time. Yet that accident irrevocably changed me and was a powerful catalyst that closed a chapter in my life. At the same time it opened new vistas.

In one cataclysmic moment I lost all emotional attachment to memories and experiences, attitudes and beliefs that, until that point had created and directed my life's program. Areas of my emotions I had been blocking were instantly cleared. I could feel again with great depth and childlike innocence.

I began to understand that if, in those lingering few seconds of that accident, I was indeed meant to die, my life's mission and my karma had been completed, and I was now free to choose whatever life I truly wanted. I became acutely aware of how we are silently drawn through our whole life by inner urges and desires born of past experiences.

Suddenly I found myself with clear 360-degree perspective of my future and past, as though I was standing on top of a mountain. The choices and directions I could take seemed vast and overwhelming. This brand new unencumbered perspective was entirely discomfiting and often confusing. Without the emotional attachments and beliefs of the past, I found myself without a point of reference to make choices or decisions.

Again I seemed angelically protected. The universe shielded my new openness and vulnerability by synchronistically attracting those people and circumstances to me that would provide comfort, protection and security until I could consciously and deliberately establish my own direction.

As a result, not only was the transition painless, my life since the accident has been filled with moments of pure magic and wonderment. For that I am filled with awe and gratitude.

However, there is a bit more to it ... That morning before the accident, I'd done a meditation to reprogram and clear my consciousness about the outcome of a past life. When I came out of the meditation, I felt much clearer and knew that I had indeed changed the past. I believe I should have died in that accident. Because I had changed the past, it changed my present and future. Interesting concept, don't you think?

Where do I go from here? For the first time in my life, I'm not sure. Former idealistic ambitions and urgent missions are gone. I am free of all desires, but one ... to love and be loved.

As I relinquish control and allow my life to unfold under the universal law of attraction, the magic and synchronicity increase. Filled with joy and anticipation, I find myself unencumbered on the brink of my dreams come true.

Isn't the universe truly amazing?

~ *Lori D'Ascenzo*

What's In A Name?

I have a friend who'd been working very hard to put on an innovative "structured networking event" for the Mississauga Board of Trade. As much as I wanted to support her, it was called for 7:00 am. My love for sleep made me question several times if I really needed to go. Each time the answer was yes.

So there I was, early morning, loading up with rubbery eggs and sitting down next to a female accountant at a round table. She looked just like you'd expect a female accountant to look, pleasant but plain, a little overweight, no make-up, neatly dressed in her navy suit, but not designer flair. I noticed her name tag said 'Jean Keene' so I made a comment to the effect that, 'Your name rhymes.'.

To which she replied in a rap beat.

"Jean Keene, the lean, mean accounting machine." I laughed because it was so incongruous with what she looked like. And the beat was catchy. But it really stuck with me – she was memorable. It tells people what she does, that she's very reasonable, no nonsense and damn good at what she does. I loved it. In answer to my questions, she described that as her tag line, something that let's people know who she is and what she does. She had learned it at some workshop. (I'd give her an A+.)

What neither of us knew, was that the guest speaker was going to describe that exact thing in different words. He wanted us to each construct a short concise sentence that we could say on the elevator or with a handshake that would tell the person who we are. Well, as I was reaching for a piece of paper in the center of the table, I distinctly heard inside: 'HELP PEOPLE CONNECT TO SOURCE.'

I dropped back into my chair and my mouth fell open. Wow! that was it. That explained not only who I am, but it explained everything I've done for the last 20 years. I was blown away and at the first break, I went out to my car in the parking lot and sat there for over an hour just letting it sink it. I cried because it had been hard to explain to others and to myself some of the stuff I had done; it had all seemed to be so fragmented up to now. But suddenly it all made sense.

By the way, 'Source' has a capital 'S' and it can mean anything you want it to.

That inner shift of knowingness must have been very powerful. Within two weeks I got a phone call out of the blue, from a stranger, with only five days notice to address a group of over 100 people in a corporate setting. It was a shock to be asked, but I got inner direction to accept it. Besides, they offered me $600 an hour.

The subject of my talk was, "Your Psychic Abilities – your way of connecting to the Collective Unconscious." I'd never addressed a group of 100 before and if you had suggested years ago that I would, I wouldn't have believed you. The beauty – the power of it all – was that it was so simple to do. The preparation just flowed and the delivery went without a hitch. I'd also been invited to speak to a smaller group of 20-30 people soon about an aspect of my spiritual journey. Both these events enable me to 'Help people connect to Source,' so they're mine to do.

My clarity of purpose is now unshakable and it acts like a filter. I joyfully approach anything that gives me an opportunity to live my purpose and pass up those things that detract or do not serve it.

~ *Lotus Lin*

Finding Courage

If one advances confidently in the direction of his dreams,
and endeavors to live the life which he has imagined, he will
meet with a success unexpected in common hours. He will
pass an invisible boundary; new, universal, and more liberal
laws will begin to establish themselves around and within him;
and he will live with the license of a high order of beings. In
proportion as he simplifies his life, the laws of the universe
will appear less complex...If you have built castles in the air,
your work need not be lost; that is where they should be.
Now put the foundations under them. ...
such is the character of that morrow which mere lapse
of time can never make to dawn.

~ Henry David Thoreau

Flying On My Own

It takes a whole village to raise a child.
- African Proverb

When I first learned I was pregnant, I cried. When I told my boyfriend, the father of my child of my condition, he left me. To add to the pressure of my already stressful situation, my family, learning I was pregnant, withdrew their support. As a result, at twenty-two years old, I found myself alone and ill-equipped to bring an infant into the world.

After my parents asked me to leave, I rented a small one-bedroom apartment and patiently waited out my pregnancy. It was the loneliest time in my life where I cried constantly. The decision I faced tore me apart; keep the baby or give him/her up for adoption.

The father refused to support me financially or emotionally and made it clear that if I contacted him or his family, he would deny the child was his and would contact Child Welfare. I was young and naive, and at the time hopelessly in love with this older, charming man, almost ten years my senior. I was devastated and feared he would make good on his threat.

What emotional strength I had left, I needed to save to care for myself so that I could get through a long and lonely pregnancy. Finally, on a cold, brisk morning, a girlfriend, whom I had met only a month earlier, and I left for the hospital in a taxi. Almost, three weeks past my due date, I was scheduled to have my labor induced. I was a mixed bag of emotions; frightened, anxious and excited all at the same time. That night February 21, 1978, I gave birth to a beautiful son, Joshua Derek Patrick. A week later, I returned from the hospital in the same taxi with my precious newborn, Joshua.

On the first night home from the hospital, I checked on my sleeping baby every five minutes. A few days later, when he grasped my finger tightly in his little fist, any remaining doubts I'd had about my decision to keep him, fled.

I quickly adapted to motherhood. Although my circumstances were tough, I learned I was tougher. Each night as I rocked Joshua to sleep, I daydreamed of a better life for us where I could be off the welfare roles and perhaps even achieve some of the dreams I'd had before I became pregnant.

Shortly after the birth, I contacted the father. I needed a snowsuit and couldn't afford one. He came over to my apartment, angrily threw some crumpled bills on the table and said that's all I was ever going to get from him. He warned me to leave him alone or else. The "or else" scared me. I couldn't risk losing my baby. I was destitute and ignorant of my rights. Joshua's father, came from a prosperous family with middle-class status,.

I stood there holding my baby and vowed to never to allow his father or anyone else to treat me so shabbily ever again.

When Joshua was two-years-old, I enrolled in the Early Childhood Education program at our local college. It was the stepping-stone I needed. Learning gave me back my self-esteem and confidence. I also took steps by becoming more involved with my community, women's groups, and my church.

Joshua and I lived on a shoe-string budget. It wasn't easy but I learned to go without, and how to stretch a dollar. I always put Joshua's needs first and despite our circumstances we somehow managed. Joshua came along while I shopped for groceries and before he was ten, he learned to read labels to determine the best buy for price and content. It was a hands-on economic education he would never receive in a classroom setting. Jason learned the rules of survival. He had a paper route and knew how to save and spend before he was nine. His paper route allowed him to buy his meals at school, save for treats, and participate in school excursions. Having his own spending money was a great help for me. It meant I could have some spare cash after paying the rent and bills.

One day at the local library I discovered the upbeat music of Rita MacNeill, the Nova Scotian recording artist. Unable to afford the purchase price, I borrowed her album, *Flying on My Own*, from the library. It seemed the music was written personally for me and I found out why when I learned Rita was also a single mother who once had the job of cleaning the stage in the same hall she later performed in. Now, Rita was a world-class singer and songwriter. She became my inspiration.

After Joshua was in bed, I would sit in my rocker and play her songs about women flying on their own. I enrolled Joshua in day-care and later in after-school programs. I hugged him a lot and I disciplined him when needed. There were times I was unemployed, and there were times I worked at two part-time jobs, but, every night at his bedtime, we gave thanks for what we had.

Over the years I made a lot friends: single and unwed women who were raising their children on their own. We all shared common ground and offered each other support over coffee and conversation. We took turns babysitting, to save money so that could have social activities beyond our children.

We unwed moms were successful in lobbying the provincial government for changes in its system that would allow single-moms better incentive programs to assist them with finding full-time employment. We became a support network. Activities included: informal gatherings, potluck meals, activities for our children and laughing, crying, and sharing each other's burdens. Collectively, we became stronger women and more confident.

I loved being Joshua's mom but parenting didn't come without a stark reminder of my past. It was especially challenging when the students in Joshua's class were asked to make Father's Day cards. How do you explain to a seven-year-old his father doesn't want to see him? I knew it was a question of time before Joshua learned the truth and that I could not protect him forever. He was a Junior High student when I arranged for him to meet his father, at Joshua's persistent request. I was more than surprised his father agreed to meet Joshua. Listening to my son sob all night, because his father told him he didn't want to have a relationship with him is the greatest pain I ever knew as a Mother. With professional counseling, Joshua eventually got over it, but I never did.

When Joshua was 15-years-old a new life began for me when I fell in love and married. But a dark cloud still hung over me. Despite my success of raising Joshua and having found my wonderful husband, the past kept haunting me. Over and over, I thought of how Joshua's father walked away, leaving me to live with the small town gossip and the task of raising a baby on my own with no support. He walked away free of any responsibility to me and his son.

Life had transformed me into a confident woman. I decided it was time to challenge Joshua's father for child support! Joshua was 16-years-old, when I finally met his father face-to-face in a legal combat. It was a nasty and long legal battle. Joshua's father and his lawyer played dirty. Big Time! But I refused to allow them to humiliate or intimidate me. Never again! I stood my ground.

My lawyer had prepared me for the discovery hearing. The only ones who would attend were the lawyers, myself, Joshua's father, and a secretary. My lawyer had warned me it would be emotionally difficult adding, and I would probably cry. I would surprise him. After the hearing we were walking back to his law office. My lawyer and I were very pleased with the outcome of the hearing but he seemed perplexed. Finally, after we reached his office he stopped and looked at me and said, "Stella, you didn't cry?" He was obviously puzzled.

I swiped his arm with my paper and quietly replied, "I cried enough when I was pregnant," and walked away smiling with a sense of pride and relief. With the emotional support of my husband, and friends combined with the legal support of my lawyer, I walked away with child support for as long as Joshua was attending school or enrolled in a secondary education program, up to the age of 21 years. An old chapter of my life was finally over. I threw up my hands, looked to the heavens and laughed with pure joy! I was free.

Joshua is now twenty-one, married and living with his with beautiful wife. I have gone on to get another degree, this time in journalism, and am proud to say I have landed a job with my local paper as a regularly featured writer. I can now truly say, I am *Flying On My Own!*

~ *Stella Shepard*

The Jewel of God

Gratitude unlocks the fullness of life. It turns what we have
into enough, and more. It turns denial into acceptance,
chaos to order, confusion to clarity. It can turn a
meal into a feast, a house into a home, a stranger into a
friend. Gratitude makes sense of our past, brings peace for
today, and creates a vision for tomorrow.
– Melody Beattie

It was Saturday and my first day home after being away for a
week on a book tour. I'd just been through the sudden break-
up of my marriage; having to sell my house in Canmore,
Alberta and was preparing to move back to the city.

After opening some of my mail, I decided to go for a hike
in the mountains near my home. I knew it was most likely
muddy and slippery on the mountain, so I removed my
special diamond ring to avoid it getting damaged or dirty if I
fell while hiking. Casually I slipped the ring off my finger and
put it on the table with my mail.

A couple of hours later, after my run, I returned home to
find a message on my answering machine from my realtor.
She told me there would be a showing the next morning. I
quickly began tidying up. The first thing I did was scoop all
the papers off my table and threw them into the garbage bag,
then headed to the garbage bin.

As I was taking the garbage out, I stopped to put my coat
on. As I did an inner nudge told me to 'open the bag and use

the big wide white twist tie that is on top the garbage.' I thought this was a pretty strange directive but being used to these inner nudges, I undid the knot in the garbage bag and opened it. Sure enough there inside was a big wide white twist tie, so I promptly tied up my garbage bag and off I went to the dumpster behind my condominium.

Later that night after going to sleep, I woke up with a start, my inner voice saying, "Look for your ring!"

The next morning I got busy early and never thought about my inner message until late afternoon. After looking for the ring, and not finding it in the usual places, I realized I had scooped it up with the papers and it had gone out in the garbage.

I wasn't concerned in the least because when I threw the garbage bag into the dumpster the night before it had been full so I knew exactly where my bag was; on top of all the others and easily accessible. No problem, I would just go out and get my bag, go through it and find my ring. Once outside though, to my surprise and shock, I saw that the garbage had been taken away! On Sunday! Who picks up garbage on Sundays?

I didn't know where to begin. The ring was worth a significant amount but the diamonds were of very special properties that couldn't be replaced. I had designed the ring myself, the middle diamond to represent my eldest son and the other two identical diamonds on either side for my twin boys. I had three children under three years of age when my marriage broke up years before and had a very close relationship to my now, young adult sons. They are the diamonds and gems of light in my life!

Unable to realize where to begin my search, a part of me wanted to give up. Just then a friend of mine called from out of town and I told her my story. She said, "You're not going to give up are you? You never give up, it's not like you."

This prompted me to take action. After saying goodbye to my friend I proceeded to call the police to see if they could help find out where the garbage was taken. I asked where the nearest landfill site was. They basically said, "Give it up lady, do you know what a land fill looks like? Call your insurance company."

I didn't want to give up even though the task at hand seemed insurmountable. Later that evening I got an inner nudge to call the town of Canmore waste disposal company. It was Sunday night and the possibility of someone being there was zero so I ignored the inner nudge for a few hours.

The feeling grew so intense that I finally looked up the number for the waste contractor, and dialed the number. A man answered and I excitedly told him my story.

He was immediately sympathetic and tried to think of many creative ways to begin the search for the ring. Never once did he say I was crazy or that I wouldn't find the ring. He said others had found things in the garbage but never anything as valuable or tiny. He also said he was heading to Calgary (a 200 kilometer round trip) at 6 am the next morning to dump the garbage truck at the landfill site.

Had I not listened to my inner guidance by calling on Sunday evening I would have missed the opportunity to look for my ring! He told me that once the trucks enter the landfill sites no one is allowed in. He did however describe the truck to me. It was 50 feet long, 10 feet high and 8 feet wide and it contained compacted garbage weighing 50 tons.

I asked him if he would call the person whose route I was on to see if he could remember approximately where in the 50-ton truck he may have dumped the bin containing my garbage bag. Ken, the waste contractor, called back and said the fellow thought he remembered dumping it in the first section of the truck. I was very excited! We now had it narrowed down to 25 tons.

He then asked what my bag looked like. I said it was black (like the other 50 tons of garbage bags).

Then I remembered that before I took the garbage out, I had followed the nudge to use the big white twist tie. Now there was a faint possibility I could identify my bag if we could locate it. The odds were incredible.

Darlene Montgomery

Ken even offered to drive the truck into Calgary, dump the rear section of his truck and bring the big truck back with the 25-ton bin of garbage that may contain my ring. He offered to help me go through it and he said it would take us about three days.

I didn't want to put him to so much expense and trouble so I asked him if I could start by my coming down before he left for Calgary at 6 am to sort through the garbage. He said sure. I will meet you and have all the lights on so you know you have the right building.

So, I had a date with Ken at 6 am, my first date all year. My realtor, a woman I barely knew, called a little later to tell me she had another showing for my home. I told her my story and without a breath of hesitation she said, "You can't do that by yourself, I'll pick you up."

I said, "Denise, you didn't hear me ... 50 tons of garbage, at 6 am, this is not something you want to do!" But she insisted.

That night I had a dream that told me my bag was on the left hand side of the truck, mid way down in the first section of the truck, about two and half feet below the surface. I had learned long ago to listen to my dreams so when Denise picked me up at 6 am I told her about my 'dream map.' She looked at me strangely but didn't say anything.

When we got to the site Ken, a very kind and gentle man met us and just said to me, "Come, let me show you what you are up against."

I looked at this 50-foot truck full of compacted garbage and I asked, " Do you have a pair of gloves I could borrow?" I proceeded to jump into the garbage truck exactly where my dream map had told me to look. Ken and Denise jumped in also. I had to keep my focus on the goal and what my dream had told me. If I had looked at the size of the job at hand I may have given up ... garbage everywhere ... tons and tons and tons!

We must have thrown a ton of garbage on the deck of the

garbage depot ... going through unbelievable things. I commented, "Boy, it's interesting what people throw away."

Ken said, "It's only garbage." Each time the pile grew too large on the deck Ken would get out of the garbage truck and take his tractor to push the garbage out of the way to make our job easier.

After searching for 40 minutes, I found the bag on the left side, mid way down, about 2.5 feet under exactly where my dream teacher had told me. But, there were holes everywhere in the bag because of the compressing of the garbage and it didn't look very hopeful. Ken came and helped me carefully lift the bag onto the deck and helped me go through it. No ring.

He said, "We'll go through it one more time, paper by paper." Then I saw a white garbage bag from my dinner three days before, containing a blue styrofoam container that had contained fish. Unfolding the compressed container I spotted my ring nestled in soft white absorbent paper inside the blue container at the very bottom of the garbage bag. The paper was soft enough to hold it and protect it from falling out. Ken and Denise stood there with mouths wide open, a look of total disbelief on their faces. I don't think either one really thought I would find it but never said so and never discouraged me from my adventure of finding it.

I asked Ken what I could do for him to thank him for all his trouble. He would accept nothing and finally I asked if I could give him a hug which he shyly accepted. I showed him the ring and he said, "Boy it was worth the effort."

I called the local newspaper and told them the story and they gave Ken and my realtor a wonderful public tribute. The paper also said that I had found the location of the ring in the 50 tons of garbage as a result of a dream.

When I called Ken's employer to find out more about him so I could buy him something that would suit him personally, his employer said, "This isn't the first time people had called to say he had been of extra service and had gone the extra mile." In my case, that extra, extra, extra mile had been through tons of garbage.

For the next week, I asked spirit with all my heart to show me the true meaning of this incredible event. Yes, it was a miracle that I found this special ring in 50 tons of garbage but I knew that I had to understand what the real message was for me. I do not believe that anything happens by coincidence.

A few nights later when I was pondering all the hidden symbols and meaning around this event, my reading light caught the middle diamond of the ring and a brilliant blue light shone from the ring. The light flooded my whole being and tears began to flow down my face. The tears came from so deep inside and they were tears of gratitude. I realized that no matter what we go through in our lives, no matter how many difficulties (symbolized by the garbage) the guidance of the Holy spirit (voice of God) and the love of God (love and help represented by the Ken and Denise) is always there with us every minute, guiding and protecting us.

What are we willing to go through to find the Jewel of God in our life? No matter what we go through, and no matter how rough life gets, we cannot give up our quest for the jewel of God, the love of family and friends and the many, many gifts in our life. I am so very grateful for the blessing of life every minute of every day.

~ *Dr. Karen Jensen*

About the Author

Darlene Montgomery is a writer, editor and respected authority on dreams who speaks to groups and organizations on uplifting subjects. Her first book published in November 1999, *Dream Yourself Awake,* chronicles the journey she took to discover her own divine mission using dreams, waking dreams and intuition.

As a consultant she helped compile two of the famous Chicken Soup books. Her stories have appeared in *Chicken Soup for the Parent's Soul* and *Chicken Soup for the Canadian Soul,* The WTN website, *Vitality Magazine* and *Synchronicity Magazine.*

Darlene's recent book media campaign took her across Canada and the U.S. where she appeared on national television and radio shows, including Michael Coren Live, Rogers Daytime, ON TV news, Breakfast Television, The Patty Purcell Show, The Life Station and more. As well Darlene operates her own public relations firm, helping to promote authors and experts.

For more on Darlene and her work visit:
www.lifedreams.org.

Other books by Darlene Montgomery

Dream Yourself Awake

This autobiography reads like a spiritual mystery. A question asked of the author by a mysterious guide sets the author on a journey to uncover the source of her deep spiritual illness and leads her to discover the one deep truth that needs to be understood for the author to be healed. Throughout the story, hundreds of personal dreams act as clues to solve the mystery, leading to the personal revelation of the author.

Dreams are a natural homing device residing in the heart of soul. Many of us are aware of a yearning or sense of destiny, purpose or mission we must find before our life is complete. In *Dream Yourself Awake*, Darlene Montgomery tells the story behind the search for her own mission in a series of dreams, waking dream and inner experiences. As we share her journey, we will discover how to use these same tools to see beyond the illusions of the mind, and travel straight to the heart of our divine purpose.

To order your copy email Darlene at:
lifedreams@idirect.com

A Message from the Publisher

In keeping with White Knight Publication's mandate to bring great titles of social concern to book and library shelves across North America, I am indeed fortunate as publisher to have been able to be closely involved with this latest publication in White Knight's "Remarkable Women Series".

Conscious Women – Conscious Lives lives up to expectations that women across North America constantly provide the nurturing component that continues to make our countries so great. These stories from across Canada and the United States of America, bring home those concerns that women have for other women providing love, nourishment and hope for our present and future generations.

Remarkable women, everyone. Thank you!

White Knight's Remarkable Women Series

Sharing MS

This informative book by the author and two women friends with Multiple Sclerosis, is a beacon of common sense lighting the way of those who have MS or suspect they may be afflicted, as well as being helpful to family, friends and health professionals. Read the book then call the MS Society Chapter in your local telephone book for information about your concerns regarding Multiple Sclerosis

ISBN 0-9730949-7-4 218 pages
US $13.95 Cdn $19.95

The Unusual Life and Times of Nancy Ford-Inman

This story is about a most remarkable woman who contributed so much to Britain's literature, the theatre, media and the war effort in spite of a major physical handicap. Badly crippled by Cerebral Palsy at an early age, she fought her way to become the author of almost 60 romantic novels and journalistic endeavors too numerous to count.

ISBN 0-9730949-8-2 238 pages
US $13.95 Cdn $19.95

To order, contact your local bookstore
or a distributor shown on the copyright page.

Contributors

BARBARA ALLPORT is a therapist in private practice in Toronto and Bancroft Ontario, Canada. She resides in Toronto with her two cats. She can be reached at b.allport@rogers.com.

LINDA C. ANDERSON is the author of *35 Golden Keys to Who You Are & Why You're Here* (Eckankar Books, 1997) and the co-author with her husband, Allen, of *God's Messengers: What Animals Teach Us about the Divine* and *Angel Animals: Exploring Our Spiritual Connection with Animals* (Plume, 1999). She and Allen co-founded the Angel Animals Network to collect and distribute stories and publish an online newsletter that is dedicated to increasing love and respect for all life (www.angelanimals.net). Linda is a national award-winning playwright and a short story and screenplay writer. She teaches inspirational writing at The Loft Literary Center in Minneapolis, Minnesota.

SUE AUGUSTINE is a dynamic conference speaker and seminar leader, and audiences world-wide describe her as invigorating, captivating and entertaining. Sue is a regular guest on national TV and radio programs and the author of the books, *"With Wings, There Are No Barriers"* (Pelican), and *"5- Minute Retreats for Busy Women"* (Harvest House), and also a contributor to *"Chicken Soup for the Women's Soul."* For more information, contact Sue at P.O. Box 2194 Niagara Falls, NY 14302; email wings@vaxxine.com; or call 905-687-8474. www.sueaugustine.com

SYBIL BARBOUR resides in Kitchener, Ontario with her husband and an aged cat. She is a retired registered nurse and midwife. She's recently fulfilled a lifelong dream of traveling to Italy, Greece, Scotland and New Zealand. You can contact her at sybilbarbour@sympatico.ca.

FRANCES BLACKWELL has traveled the world as a speaker and workshop facilitator. She specializes in designing and delivering workshops on spiritual topics. In her career, she worked in Women's Health Services with the Planned Parenthood division as a community outreach worker and clinical assistant. You can reach Fran at: frannb@adelphia.net.

JOAN BORYSENKO, PH.D. is a leading expert on stress, spirituality, and the mind/body connection. She has a doctorate in medical sciences from Harvard Medical School, is a licensed clinical psychologist, and president of Mind-Body Health Sciences, LLC. An internationally known speaker and consultant in women's health and spirituality, integrative medicine, life balance, and the mind/ body connection, she is the author of eleven books, including the New York Times bestseller *Minding the Body, Mending the Mind*, two 1-hour videos, and numerous best-selling audiocassette programs. Her nine books are a complete library of healing, combining scholarly wisdom with the language of the heart, and bringing body and soul together with unprecedented clarity and sophistication. Dr. Borysenko's work has appeared in numerous scientific journals and has been featured in many popular magazines and newspapers. She has appeared on Oprah, Sally Jesse Raphael, Sonya Live, Geraldo, Hour Magazine and Good Morning America among others. Her work has been featured in US News and World Report, the Wall Street Journal, USA Today, Reader's Digest, Success, Bottom Line, The Leifer Report, American Health, Shape, Glamour, Vogue, Ladies Home Journal, Living Fit, Success, Yoga Journal, New Age Journal, and many other magazines and newspapers. To learn more visit www.joanborysenko.com

ANNE ARCHER BUTCHER is a well-known international speaker and has addressed thousands of people in the USA, Europe, Canada, Africa, Australia and New Zealand. She is a radio host, a published writer and an award-winning video producer. Anne and her husband, Alden, own Dolphin Entertainment Company, producing films that uplift, educate and inspire. Her clients have included top celebrities as well as President Gerald Ford. She also works with corporate clients on marketing and communications. Anne has her Master's Degree in English and Education and was an Advanced Placement Scholar who attended high school in France and Germany.

MEDEA BEVARELLA CHECKIK has been practicing transformational Psychotherapy in Toronto, Ontario, for the last ten years. She facilitates workshops on "The Self in Transformation." Medea incorporates meditation, mindfulness, spiritual awareness and energy balancing both in her private practice and in groups. Her work is a reflection of her extensive knowledge and wisdom as well as her evolving spiritual presence. To contact Medea call 416-530-1956 or email her at: medeasatya@sympatico.ca.

BRENDA CHISHOLM lives in Burlington, Ontario, with her husband, Robin, and two daughters, Kendra and Marina Grace. She works full-time in a software company; writes in the evenings for an on-line community magazine; has a weird record collection of 45 rpms from the 70s and 80s, and, enjoys singing. You can reach Brenda at (905) 639-4568.

DARYL CLARKE has expressed herself creatively since birth through music, art and words. She has been published in *The Toronto Star* and periodicals throughout North America. Founder of the *Spirited Woman Magazine* and Healing Rock Retreat on the shores of Lake Huron in Tobermory, Ontario, Daryl cherishes her life journey while helping others stay connected to their spirit. Her address is 417 Eagle Road, Tobermory, Ontario, Canada, N0H 2R0 and her web site is www.spiritedwoman.com.

LORI D'ASCENZO is an Esoteric Astrologer specializing in the evolution of soul. The publisher of Beyond Reason magazine and a dynamic writer and speaker on metaphysical and holistic health related topics, Lori has appeared many times on radio and television. She can be reached at mediaart@cogeco.ca or visit her website www.beyondreason.com.

ERIN DAVIS was born in Edmonton, Alberta and as a result of her father's Air Force career, was raised in many places, including Ottawa, Trenton and Britain. Erin's introduction to show business came at an early age when she sang regularly with her grandfather's orchestra. Her love of performing led her to study Radio Broadcasting at Loyalist College in Belleville, Ontario. By her second year, she was hosting an afternoon radio show on CIGL FM.

Upon graduation on the Dean's List, Erin moved to Windsor, Ontario and began reading morning news on CKLW, The Big Eight. Shortly after, she became the first female morning co-host in the powerful Detroit market. A station format change led Erin to move to Toronto, where she co-hosted the morning show on All News Radio CKO for four years. Her big break came in the summer of 1988 when the call came for her to do morning news on the popular Daynard Drive-In on 98.1 CHFI. The chemistry between Erin and host Don Daynard was magical and she soon became Don's co-host...a partnership that became hugely popular over their eleven years together until Don's retirement. Erin continued to host the CHFI morning show until the spring of 2003.

Following a number of guest-host positions at CFTO and Global, Erin wrote and performed a nightly commentary on CFTO News in 1998 and 1999 called *Just So You Know*. Then, for two seasons, she hosted a nightly talk show (more than 200 episodes) on Rogers Television called *The Erin Davis Show*. The lifestyle and wellness program, which was seen in over two million homes in Southern Ontario, received an award in its second season as Canada's best cable talk show. In 2002, Erin was honored by being named the year's first *Chatelaine* Woman Of Influence, joining the ranks of such luminaries as Former Prime Minister Kim Campbell, Indigo chief Heather Reisman, Astronaut Roberta Bondar and fellow broadcaster Pamela Wallin. Erin writes a daily internet journal, available at www.erindavis.com.

NANCY LEE DOIGE lives in Aurora, Ontario, Canada, where she developed a national education program on transplantation and organ donation for grade five through eight students. The Classroom Connections "Gift of Life" Education Program is currently in 7,500 schools across Canada. Nancy draws on her education in family studies at Ryerson University, her work with children in elementary schools and her deeply moving experience when her son Ryan died. Visit her at www.classroom-connections.com or www.ryanshope.net.

ARLENE FORBES is a Registered nurse. She combines 24 years of experience in multiple areas of nursing with her spiritual studies and her creativity as an interpretive dancer of music and poetry to create healing environments for her clients, as well as large audiences worldwide. She is an aspiring writer of fiction and inspirational stories. She lives in Minneapolis Minnesota with her husband, Aubrey. You can reach Arlene at eagleforbes@qwest.net.

DR. KAREN JENSEN ND received her degree in naturopathic medicine from the Canadian College of Naturopathic Medicine (CCNM) in Ontario in 1988. Dr. Jensen served of the board of the Ontario Naturopathic Association and held a three year position on the board of the Canadian Naturopathic Association and is past President of the Alberta Naturopathic Association. Her clinical focus has been women's health, immune disorders, learning disorders, allergies, cardiovascular health, sports medicine, chronic fatigue syndrome, energy medicine and children' health. Dr. Jensen is a well-known lecturer and appears regularly on television and radio. She writes extensively for health magazines across Canada. She has written the book *Menopause: A Naturopathic Approach to the Transitional Years* and is the co-author of the new book NO MORE HRT: Menopause, Treat the Cause and The Complete Athlete. For more information visit www.drkarenjensen.com

KAHLEE KEANE – Root Woman, is an educator and eco-herbalist. Her lectures, books, videos and herbology courses stress the sustainable use of medicinal plants while teaching others to make and use the medicines that are their birthright. She is the founder of Senega Watch (branch of Save Our Species). Kahlee and David Howarth have just published *The Standing People* , a guide to the medicinal wild plants found in Canada. Web site is www.connect.to /rootwoman . Her e-mail is rootwoman@sasktel.net, and mail address, Box #27 2001 - 8th St. E., Saskatoon, Saskatchewan S7H OT8

SHEILA KINDELLAN-SHEEHAN is a native of Québec. She holds an MA in English from Concordia University. Her work has been published in *Room of One's Own, The Globe and Mail,* read on *CBC's First Person Singular, Radio One, CBC Montreal, and CJAD. Sheila's Take,* her first collection of short stories, a *Shoreline* publication in 2003, has twice been cited on the bestseller list. Ms Kindellan is also a popular speaker on the Québec circuit.

NANCY LACASSE of Mississauga, Ontario, married her high school sweetheart, Norm, and the pride of her life are their two teenage daughters, Lanna & Tabitha. Throughout the past 15 years, Nancy has received the Community Entrepreneur of the Month Award for promoting Children's Character Building Music Programs. She is a Certified Toastmaster (CTM - International Public Speaking Organization) with awards for Public Speaking. She has received numerous Community Awards, media appearances, and letters of thanks for organizing large Children's Health and Safety events. Nancy appeared on Children's Miracle Network Telethon, and has been a fundraising & marketing consultant. She works as a Health Care Research Specialist/Broker and a Certified Tax Advisor, representing unique Family Health and Tax Saving Programs from award winning Usana Health Sciences Inc. and Benecaid Health Benefit Solutions Inc. www.unitoday.net/nlacasse. Her life's mission is to help save children from disease by educating families of the dangers of toxins to children's health and teaching parents everything she's learned about all the alternatives, products and services available to help them financially and to help raise healthy, confident children.

SUZANNE THOMAS LAWLOR is the Director of Education and Public Relations for Humanity in Unity, a nonprofit organization dedicated to bringing relief and upliftment to all races, cultures and religions. Suzanne lives in the San Francisco Bay area and continues her work as a freelance writer. For the last 30 years she has taught meditation and studied the development of consciousness through Vedic and Eastern traditions. Along the way her life has been graced by many travels and many teachers, including Maharishi Mahesh Yogi and a handful of extraordinary Divine Mothers who reflect the Truth that: God is both Father and Mother. She is currently working on a book on the Kathars, the mystical branch of Christianity founded by Mary Magdalene. Suzanne can be contacted at riverofgrace@aol.com.

CAROL LE NEVEU is a holistic career and life coach, metaphysician and dynamic speaker. After several years as a family lawyer in downtown Toronto, Carol left the practice to pursue her dream of helping others discover their purpose and find more meaning in their lives. You can contact Carol at 416-960-8188.

LOTUS LIN has retired from 30 years in the investment industry. Lotus currently has a variety of business interests that advance personal and organizational consciousness. She is a trained psychotherapist certified in several healing modalities, including Reiki Master. She provides healing energy through Lotus treatments as seva. For more information email lotuslin@cogeco.ca.

JANET MATTHEWS is a writer, editor, speaker, teacher and co-author of the Canadian Bestseller, *Chicken Soup for the Canadian Soul*. Janet has been a guest on countless television and radio talk shows across Canada, and doing guest speaking spots and interviews. Janet is also working with Daniel Keenan to produce a book-sized version of *"The Navy's Baby,"* a wonderfully inspiring story that appears in *Chicken Soup for the Parent's Soul*. You can contact Janet at: Chicken Soup for the Canadian Soul, 2- 9225 Leslie Street, Richmond Hill Ontario, L4B 3H6 or call: 905-881-8995 ext 28.

DEBBIE MCMECHAN describes herself as a child of the southwest Manitoba prairies. Together with her husband, Tony, and three children, Danielle, Justin and Paige, she makes her living off the land, raising cattle and growing crops.

MARY CARROLL MOORE has been a published writer since 1977. Her essays, articles, columns, and stories have been in over 200 publications, including *American Artist, Health, Prevention*, the *Boston Globe*, the *Los Angeles Times*, and many other national media. Mary writes a bimonthly food column for the *Los Angeles Times* syndicate, which appears in over 86 newspapers nationwide, and a bimonthly column for the *Minneapolis Star-Tribune*. Ten of her nonfiction books are published and she just finished her first fiction book, *Breathing Room*, a collection of linked stories. Art has been an important part of Mary's healing from breast cancer. Although Mary minored in painting in college and studied with different teachers, it wasn't until 1999, when she began studying pastel painting, that she really understood the power of color and light. She became a student of full-color seeing, attending classes with teacher and artist Susan Sarback at The School of Light and Color in Fair Oaks, California. For more about Mary and her work visit www.marycarrollmoore.com.

DARLENE MONTGOMERY is an internationally respected authority on dreams, spiritual perspectives and ideas. She is an author, speaker and clergywoman who speaks to groups and organizations on uplifting subjects. Her first book, *Dream Yourself Awake*, published in 1999, chronicles the journey she took to discover her own divine mission. Her stories have appeared in *Chicken Soup for the Parent's Soul, Chicken Soup for the Canadian Soul*, WTN website, ECKANKAR Writers Newsletter. She lives in Toronto, Ontario. Email her at lifedreams@idirect.com.

BARBARA O'CONNELL lives in Boston, Massachusetts with her husband Patrick, and two children, William and Paige. She has been executive in the software industry for over 20 years. Barbara is a speaker and facilitator on spiritual and business topics internationally.

CAROL MATTHEWS-O'CONNOR is a daughter/ mother/ wife/friend/cook/animal lover/children's book author/and second-grade teacher in a migrant farm worker town in South Florida where she enjoys grand adventures with her students. She has published two beginning reader picture books. Children's literature tops the list of her favorite things, along with riding horses, hiking mountain trails (especially in the West), music, and cooking for friends.

PATRICIA ORWIN resides in Comox, British Columbia. where she works in the health food industry assisting others in taking charge of their health on all levels. She has always felt a deep connection to nature, which inspires her love of writing inspirational poetry. You can contact Patricia at patriciaorwin@yahoo.ca.

MARINA QUATTROCCHI Ph.D has worked as a photojournalist and teacher in primary and secondary schools. She completed a masters and doctoral degree in educational psychology. After 17 years of teaching she burned out from severe migraines so has spent many years trying to rise out of the ashes and balance her life. She's developed a series of workshops called Journey of Awareness that help participants live with greater balance, harmony and joy in their lives. Her workshops teach participants how to understand their dreams, break through illusions and balance their energy. She also does individual dream therapy and the Myers-Briggs personality inventory. She's an avid reader, who enjoys yoga, Tai Chi, biking, the gym and spending time with her cat Small Fry. Her e-mail address is marina.quattro@sympatico.ca

ELIZABETH BETTY RICE has been a Master Teacher for over 25 years, currently back in the classroom as instructor to determine the academic needs of today's youth and to personally assess their reading skills. She was instrumental in instituting the "RICE Reading Program" (RICE stands for: Reading Is Confidential and Essential), a program to increase reading and comprehension scores. Elizabeth is also Co-Founder and President of Tomorrows' World Foundation Inc., a non-profit organization stressing educational, social, spiritual, physical and financial empowerment with a focus on African Americans and other minorities. She resides in Washington DC with her husband.

YALONDE SAVOIE lives in Toronto, Ontario and is a singer, song-writer for children and adults. She also has a business organizing lives, offices and homes.

STELLA SHEPPARD lives on an organic farm on beautiful Prince Edward Island, Canada, with her husband and best friend, Reg Phelan. In 2000, Stella graduated from Holland College, Prince Edward Island with a degree in Journalism. She is a researcher and freelance writer who is published regularly in Maritime agricultural, forestry, and fishing newspapers. She writes a monthly newspaper column: *Life On The Farm*, for The Island Harvest, a Prince Edward Island publication. Her story, The Red Sweater, was published in *Chicken Soup for the Canadian Soul* (2002). Stella and Reg are social activists involved in community and international develop-ment work. Her son, Joshua, is married and has chosen to live on Prince Edward Island. Reach Stella at rphelan@pei.sympatico.ca.

JUDY POLLARD SMITH has been writing in various forms for many years, including Book Reviews for *The Hamilton Spectator*, free-lance commentaries for the *Globe and Mail*, author interviews which have appeared in the *Hamilton Spectator* and in *The Women Writer* in the U. K., and educational workbooks. She has held memberships in The Trollope society, The Kilvert Society (UK), The Barbara Pym Society of North America. She enjoys full membership in The Society of Women Writers and Journalists in Britain, The Hamilton Quill Club, and meets regularly with a small group of friends to discuss books. She enjoys judging The Power of the Pen teen writing contest every year for the Hamilton Public Library and teaches English as A Second Language to adults for the Hamilton Board of Education. She lives with her husband John and their three University-aged children, Hayley, Drew and Jock, and their Airedale "Niko".

HEATHER THOMPSON is an award winning professional broadcaster, with 27 years experience in media and public relations. Born in Sudbury, Ontario, Canada, Heather spent her early years in North Bay and then Huntsville. After a completing a year of university with plans to be a teacher, she made the switch to a Radio Television Course to earn a diploma from Canadore College in North Bay. Heather was the first female recipient of the News Director of the Year Award from Telemedia Communications. She was also named Employee of the Year by Telemedia for efforts in creating an employee liaison committee with the company. She is the recipient of three awards of merit from the Ontario Provincial Police Association (OPPA), two regional and one provincial, recognizing her spot news and feature programming on policing. Heather actively assists with on-going media workshops at OPP headquarters in Orillia. Heather has also received numerous certificates of appreciation for her assistance with charities and organizations. She served two terms as Central Canada Regional Director for the Radio Television News Director's Association of Canada (RTNDA).

Heather is currently the News Director morning show co-host for Rogers Radio at 105.9 Jack F-M in Orillia. She has lived in the Sunshine City for seven years. With her brother Brent, they jointly purchased and live in the "Vick" house, one of the original Victorian style houses built by the Vick family, early entrepreneurs in the city. She is a collector of things dealing with cats, angels, teddy bears and Coca Cola . She can be reached at heather.thompson@rogers.com.

MARION WOODMAN is a writer, international teacher and workshop leader, and Jungian analyst. With over a half-million copies in print, she is one of the most widely read authors on analytical and feminine psychology of our times. Marion Woodman is a graduate of the C.G. Jung Institute in Zurich. Her best selling book *Addiction to Perfection* is considered to be a landmark study on the spiritual and psychological roots of addiction in women. Some of her other books include *The Ravaged Bridegroom; Leaving My Father's House; The Maiden King;* and *The Pregnant Virgin.* Her newest book, *Bone : Dying into Life* (Viking Press, September 2000) is the story of her dealing with and healing from uterine cancer and transforming her life in the process. For more about Marion visit www.mwoodmanfoundation.org.

Permissions

A *Glimpse of My Mother's Soul*. Reprinted by permission of Carol Matthews O'Connor © Carol Matthews O'Connor 2003

A *Love Everlasting*. Reprinted by permission of Suzanne Lawlor © Suzanne Lawlor 1996

An *Everlasting Farewell*. Reprinted by permission of Marion Woodman © Marion Woodman 2003

Another Chance at Life. Reprinted by permission of Elizabeth Rice © Elizabeth Rice 2002

Bathroom Humor. Reprinted by permission of Heather Thompson © Heather Thompson 2003

Becoming Conscious. Reprinted by permission of Daryl Clarke © Daryl Clarke 2001

Cleansing by Fire. Reprinted by permission of Marina Quattrocchi © Marina Quattrocchi 2000

Finding My Wings. Reprinted by permission of Sue Augustine © Sue Augustine 1996

Finding My Own Medicine. Reprinted by permission of Kahlee Keane © Kahlee Keane 2001

Flying On My Own. Reprinted by permission of Stella Shepard © Stella Shepard 2002

Gifts from a Dying Sister. Reprinted by permission Of Medea Bavarella Chechik © Medea Bavarella Chechik 2001